# CHALLENGE YOUR IQ

THIS IS A CARLTON BOOK

Text and puzzle content © British Mensa Limited 1998, 2005
Design and Artwork © Carlton Books Limited 1998, 2005

This edition published by Carlton Books Limited 2005
20 Mortimer Street
London W1T 3JW

A CIP catalogue for this book is available from the British Library.

ISBN 184442 432 4

Printed and bound in India

**MENSA** ®
THE HIGH IQ SOCIETY

# CHALLENGE YOUR IQ

John Bremner    Philip Carter    Ken Russell

CARLTON

Mensa is the international society for people with a high IQ. We have more than 100,000 members in over 40 countries worldwide.

The society's aims are:
> to identify and foster human intelligence for the benefit of humanity
> to encourage research in the nature, characteristics, and uses of intelligence
> to provide a stimulating intellectual and social environment for its members

Anyone with an IQ score in the top two per cent of population is eligible to become a member of Mensa – are you the 'one in 50' we've been looking for?

Mensa membership offers an excellent range of benefits:
> Networking and social activities nationally and around the world
> Special Interest Groups – hundreds of chances to pursue your hobbies and interests – from art to zoology!
> Monthly members' magazine and regional newsletters
> Local meetings – from games challenges to food and drink
> National and international weekend gatherings and conferences
> Intellectually stimulating lectures and seminars
> Access to the worldwide SIGHT network for travellers and hosts

For more information about Mensa: www.mensa.org, or

**British Mensa Ltd.,**
St John's House,
St John's Square,
Wolverhampton
WV2 4AH
Telephone: +44 (0) 1902 772771
E-mail: enquiries@mensa.org.uk
www.mensa.org.uk

**Mensa Canada**
PO Box 1570,
Kingston, ON.
K7L 5C8
Voice: 613-547-0824
Fax:    613-531-0626
E-mail: mensa@eventsmgt.com
www.canada.mensa.org

# Contents

# About Intelligence

Intelligence has many definitions. In 1923 it was wryly defined by the psychologist Edwin Boring as "That quality which intelligence tests measure." And things are exactly as simple and as complex as that. IQ — our intelligence quotient — is a difficult thing to pin down. IQ tests are scorned by some as testing only the ability to do IQ tests, but many of the abilities involved in the completion of IQ tests have proven to be very useful in our daily lives. The various abilities of logical thinking, problem solving, dealing with the language that we use every day, and manipulating numbers and shapes are the same abilities which, when combined with emotional reasoning, make us effective human beings.

Another psychologist, Ulric Neisser, recently defined intelligence around the concept of an *ideal prototype*, with people being more or less intelligent according to how closely they approach the prototype. There are two ways of achieving a prototype. The psychometric prototype is statistical where we simply say that a perfect score is 1 and this becomes the ideal prototype. We are scored according to our deviation from that score. This is close to the method used to score most IQ tests currently in use where the IQ score is the deviation of a person's score on a test from the mean test score of a reference population, divided by the standard deviation. In other words, the rating which you achieve on an IQ test is compared with the rating which everyone else achieves, and your score is weighted according to the results of others. By definition according to the convention of scoring, the average IQ is 100, and we know that fifty percent of the population will score between 90 and 110. But if, on a particular test, it were found that the average of all tested was 90, the weighting would be adjusted to bring the average back up to 100. Thus are tests standardized. Looking at the sample figures below it can be seen that if all points were plotted, the classic bell-shaped curve would be evident. More on that later.

50% of the population have IQs between 90 and 110. Only 2% have IQs lower than 53 or higher than 147

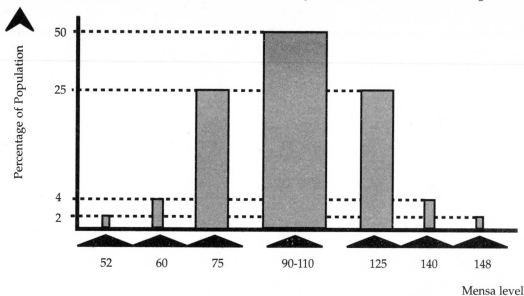

The other way of achieving a prototype is to define the ideal intelligence in terms of cognitive-psychology, where intelligence is viewed as a process. To do this we would have to choose the ideal processes of intelligence such as problem definition, memory storage, mental imaging, resource collection, and problem solving, and we would also have the dilemma of having to define the ideal prototype use for that intelligence. But the processes are complex and infinitely varied according to the type of problem being solved and we can be specific only to the environment in which we operate. Solving the problem of, (say) stopping somebody from shouting at you, involves few of the processes of defining the difference between (say) paper and metal foil. As to environments, a physics genius may have the ideal intelligence for making discoveries about relativity or quantum mechanics, but be unable to survive in a desert where the average nomad who has never heard of physics, thrives happily. But take the nomad out of the desert into a physics laboratory and the situation is reversed.

Perhaps with something like the above example in mind, intelligence has been defined by H. Woodrow as "The capacity to acquire capacity;" by S.S. Colvin as "The ability to adjust oneself to the environment;" and by R. Pintner as "The ability to adapt oneself adequately to relatively new situations in life." In other words, if the nomad is an intelligent nomad, he will be able to learn about physics, given the opportunity and inclination, and if the physics professor finds himself in the desert, if he is an intelligent physics professor and comes under the instruction of a group of nomads, he will be able to learn the things necessary for survival.

## Types of Intelligence

What Woodrow, Colvin and Pintner all seem to be identifying has come to be known as *fluid intelligence* — the combination of qualities measured by the Cattell test used by Mensa, and the same qualities which have ensured our survival as a species and the lack of which causes the downfall of species less able to adapt to changing circumstances. This combined intelligence aspect has great relevance in everyday life, particularly in today's changing jobmarket. Versatility is the most important asset of potential employees. What you are capable of now matters more than what you have done in the past. There have been a number of cases where very high fliers have been enticed away, for huge sums of money, from jobs where they were achieving spectacular success, in the hope that they could bring that success with them and turn failing businesses into successes, only for them to become equally spectacular failures in their new positions. Where did things go wrong? Why cannot future success be measured by past performance?

The answer is that it may have taken years for them to learn how to be good at their last job, and during those years they will have accumulated judgement, wisdom, and thinking skills specific to that job and situation. But in the case of those somewhat lacking in fluid intelligence, only specific to that situation. Their new employers have failed to realize that someone who has spent the last twenty years learning about (say) steel may have achieved that success by hard work and determination and by learning the hard way — from mistakes. A better way to choose a new company leader who would not spend the first five years learning from mistakes would be to test the fluid intelligence of every reliable and hard-working employee already working for the company and promote the person with the highest score into the position! Well, perhaps not, but the lesson should be learned that people can have achieved success despite being dull thinkers and perhaps in some cases because of it. Traditional methods usually work for someone who knows what to do, but ask the same person to do original thinking or to apply old methods to a new situation, and chaos can result.

Thus, in the workplace, the ability to learn a new job is more important than what the applicant already knows. Most employers who understand this, and who require thinking skills and judgement as employment prerequisites, have moved from measuring general and acquired knowledge — which is really a measure of memory and past experience, to IQ tests, which are a better measure of future learning ability and judgement.

Unfortunately though, fluid intelligence is not perfectly measured by psychometric IQ tests. Flexible and effective managers may not always have high IQ ratings, but they know how to deal with people, sort out problems, make fast decisions, and perhaps keep a factory in all its complexity in operation. Aptitude and personality tests may also be necessary. As another example, to obtain their taxi licence, taxi drivers in London need to have acquired 'the knowledge' — a mental map of London which enables them to go by the shortest or fastest route from *a* to *b* anywhere in the city.

Few of these taxi drivers are likely to have astonishingly high psychometric IQs, and their intelligence may not be truly fluid, but they have very high knowledge-based intelligence specific to their job, which takes a great deal of hard work and determination to acquire and which gives them an advantage over other drivers in London who may have much higher psychometric intelligence. There will be also be some crossover of their skills and acquired intelligence into everyday life. Visual-spatial intelligence — which taxi drivers must necessarily acquire, is thought by many experts to be the aspect of intelligence which gives the most accurate score of natural non-culture-based intelligence. In the case of taxi drivers, this may not always hold true, but it is likely that their increased visual-spatial skills will have the effect of increasing their overall IQ score.

But like the brilliant manager or company director with knowledge-based crystallized intelligence who is recruited by another company, if the taxi driver were transported to a strange city he would be less effective for a considerable time than the locals. The taxi driver's job-specific intelligence does not have the same survival value as the previously mentioned nomad's fluid intelligence. That said, knowledge-based intelligence is highly valued by our society and is of more value to an individual who uses it than high psychometric IQ to an individual who does not use that potential. In the end, what we do with our intelligence matters more than the type or quantity of intelligence we have at our disposal.

## Divergent and convergent thinking

If you have good fluid intelligence, you will be good at divergent thinking — the process of finding previously undiscovered solutions to problems, whatever the type of problem you tackle. It can take the same kind of creative intelligence to find a workable solution to a family crisis as to find a cure for a disease, or to invent a new type of engine. The tools you need to solve problems with divergent thinking are originality, adaptability, fluency, and inventiveness, and the typical divergent thinker will usually explore many possible solutions before finding the best one. It may even be true to say that only a divergent thinker can do this.

A convergent thinker is likely to pick the first viable solution that is found, and stick to that no matter what happens. Divergent thinkers have multi-track minds. Convergent thinkers have one-track minds. Henry Ford's famous slogan about the model T Ford, "You can have any color so long as it is black," is typical of a convergent thinker, but Ford was a good convergent thinker, so he surrounded himself with divergent thinkers and he had a row of buzzers on his desk to summon the thinkers he needed to solve his problems. Again typical of convergent thinkers, Ford was very stubborn. Despite being told that an eight cylinder V8 engine block was technically impossible, he instructed his engineers to design and make the engine and he repeatedly refused to take no for an answer. He had picked his first viable solution and nothing was going to change his mind. It took over a year for his design team — divergent thinkers to a man — to come up with a solution, but when they did it took the motoring world by storm. The force of combined divergent and convergent thinking working together is hard to beat.

## Physical Changes

Contrary to popular belief, the brain undergoes physical changes in the process of learning. We can't make more brain cells, but we constantly make new connections between those cells in a network many thousand times more complex than the world wide telephone network. Knowledge increases that network of connections as does acquired skill and improved mental capacity of every kind. Recent studies have shown that even fluid intelligence can be improved by exercising the brain. Each cell in our brain can have up to 10,000 connections, some of which

Skills and knowledge are mapped onto brain cells connected by axons which are protected by myelin sheathing.

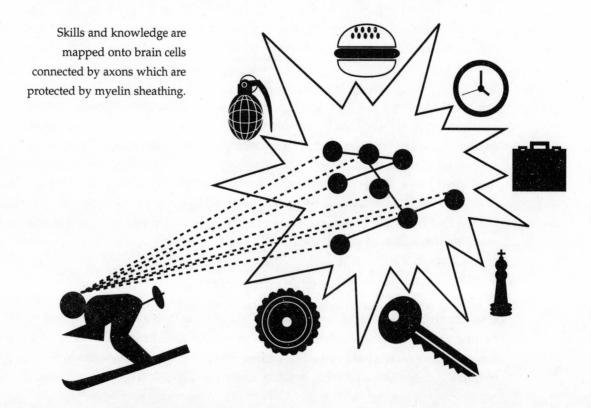

get priority over others. When we use a connection route a lot — when we learn things permanently — our brain decides to protect that connection and coats the connections with myelin, enabling faster and more reliable chemical and electrical communication. Thus, old people with Alzheimer's disease, who have forgotten everything they have learned over the past sixty years, may still be able to recall verses learned by rote in childhood, the memories protected from the ravages of Alzheimer's by myelin sheathing. Thus also, recurrent nightmares and bad memories. When something terrible happens to us, our brain ensures that we don't forget it by coating the relevant connections in myelin. This is a defense mechanism to try to prevent recurrence of the harmful circumstance. But these are mapped into cerebellum; not really like cerebral memories above (in these examples, the cerebellum at the base of the brain).

This also explains why exciting lessons are easier to learn that boring ones. The brain does not invest much construction time creating new connections or protecting connections for things that apparently do not matter. Everything that happens in the brain is a matter of survival priorities. Only if something matters to us so much that we keep returning to it does the brain build protected connections to that information or skill. This is why very slow readers, like those with dyslexia, who keep having to go back over the material, when they do get through a book, know it much better than a fast reader who looked at each word only once. Because of their very short term memory for words, some dyslexic people have to learn each sentence as we would learn a poem by heart, a few words at a time. Only when they have memorized the whole sentence in this way do they make sense of it, but to do this their brain must invest in some myelin engineering. Dyslexic actors, once they have learned their lines, are most unlikely to forget them.

Learning by rote, sneered at by many, has its uses, and not just for people who are dyslexic. We can all make use of myelin engineering.

## Music

A study by neurological scientists at the Universities of Wisconsin and California, of 78 three and four-year-olds from various social and economic backgrounds, showed them performing 34 per cent better than other children in IQ tests after being given simple piano lessons for six months. This is myelin engineering in action. The children appear to have gained their IQ advantage by the exercise of translating notes on paper into music on the keyboard. This is a vital time for the creation of neural networks — the pathways of our thinking. The repetitive nature of learning music seems to give just the right kick-start to the growth and myelization of the vital axons that communicate with other parts of our brain responsible for spatial-temporal reasoning. Quite why music should have this effect, nobody yet knows, but it makes sense to take advantage of such a massive IQ boosting effect — on its own enough to more than compensate for many other disadvantages.

## Genetic Components and the Bell Curve

Around 60% of our IQ potential is inherited from our parents. The remainder is affected by social and environmental factors such as living conditions, parental encouragement and mental stimulation, access to learning materials, such as in the music effect above, and nutrition. It is less likely, for example, for poor people to have access to a piano. People who lead less privileged lifestyles, wherever they live, tend to have lower average IQ levels. Animal studies have also shown that the growth of dendrites and axons in the brain — the wiring of the brain network — is dependent upon these environmental factors. Without the wiring in place our brain cells cannot communicate with each other — we cannot think. However, since our IQ can be damaged by the environment in which our brain has to operate, it follows that it can be enhanced by improving those conditions and in fact we can see this taking place. As social conditions improve throughout the developed world we see a rise in IQ levels. We may be smarter as a race and as we get smarter, it may be more likely that we pass smarter genes down to our children and the cycle continues. Good so far, but a snag arises with this cycle. A healthy lifestyle in today's world is mostly achieved through wealth. We are forced to the conclusion that the wealthy will be getting smarter while the poor will not. Recent controversy has entered this arena with the publication in 1994 of *The Bell Curve* by Herrnstein and Murray.

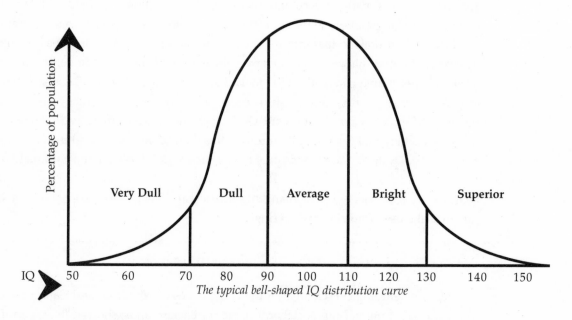

*The typical bell-shaped IQ distribution curve*

Based upon long term accumulation of psychometric IQ test information and upon a survey of more than 12,000 people from all social groups in the USA between the ages of 14 and 22, Herrnstein and Murray have come to the conclusion that the intelligence bipolarization is actually happening and will continue to accelerate unless we take drastic action to stop it. The book raised a storm because people do not like this conclusion. Politicians do not like it because they are, to a large extent, responsible for the living conditions of our society. The poor do not like it because it shows them to be less intelligent. Ethnic minorities do not like it because in some societies they are among the poorest and controversial claims have been made that the cause of the IQ differential is ethnic rather than wealth based. The wealthy do not like it because they would have to pay more tax to improve the living conditions of poor people.

In the end what matters is not whether people like the conclusion, but whether it is true and if so, what can be done to solve the problem. Unfortunately there is no easy solution. The poverty trap is also to some extent an IQ trap. British Mensa's recent census of members showed that the unemployment figure for Mensans is less than half the national average. Since Mensa is discrimination-free — passing a tough supervised test is the only way in — Mensans are a fairly representative sample of the top 2% of the population. This means that the less intelligent you are, the more likely you are to be unemployed — in other words, low IQ leads to poverty. Here then is the so-called Catch-22 — poverty leads to low IQ. Thus the concerns raised by *The Bell Curve*. For those in the poverty trap there seems no way out. To get out they need higher IQs. To have higher IQs they need, according to Herrnstein and Murray, to be wealthier.

This isn't strictly true because we know that about 8% of those in Mensa have incomes that are either close to the poverty line or below it, so just as it is possible to be wealthy and intellectually challenged, it is possible to be intelligent and poor. Thus, looking at the population as a whole, if Mensa is representative of the distribution of intelligence and poverty in society, we can extrapolate that perhaps 0.16% of the population will have Mensa level intelligence and be living in poverty.

Compare that to the 13.9% in the USA, who in 1996, according to the Economic Policy Unit, were earning at or below poverty level wages. In the UK the poverty figure is variously estimated at between 18% and 25%, but the European criteria is different, with the poverty line estimated as half of the average wage rather than at a minimum hourly income level as in the USA.

However we arrive at the figures it is clear that you are much less likely to be poor if you have an IQ in the top 2% of the population, and it would be a fair assumption to say that the more intelligent you are, the less likely you are to be living in poverty. Thus, we are forced to the conclusion, like Herrnstein and Murray, that to get rid of the *poverty equals low IQ equals poverty* cycle, we need to improve society.

## Unmeasurable IQ

It is not possible to measure musical aptitude or artistic talent in a standard IQ test. Neither is it possible, through an IQ test, to measure the many and various craft talents and skills — some of which require very sophisticated thinking. A carpenter, beauty consultant, printer or hairdresser needs to be able to look at any job, estimate its cost and how long it will take, work out the materials required, figure out how to do the job, and then negotiate with the person who wants the work done. The job has to be skilfully completed, working with a variety of different tools and materials and in many cases the person undertaking the work will have a greater understanding of the practicalities of the job than others with less skill but much higher measurable IQ ratings. In Scotland there is an architect who designed a roof in such a way that it could only be constructed if it were put in place before the building which was supposed to support it. The builder redesigned the roof with the comment that the architect was "All brains and no common sense."

## Individual Strengths and Weaknesses

Working through this book you may discover that you have greater numerical than verbal skills, or that your ability to work with shapes — *visual-spatial intelligence* — is your greatest strength. We each have individual strengths and weaknesses. The important thing is to recognize our own abilities and apply ourselves to the things that we do best. Many talented writers claim to be hopeless with numbers, and there are mathematicians who cannot spell and surgeons who have brilliant memories and wonderful visual-spatial ability but who cannot operate a video recorder. This book will help you to recognize your strengths and weaknesses.

## Look at the following problems and see which you can do most easily:

*(Answers at the end of this chapter.)*

### Visual-Cognitive

All blocks not on the bottom row
are supported by blocks
underneath.

How many blocks?

**1**

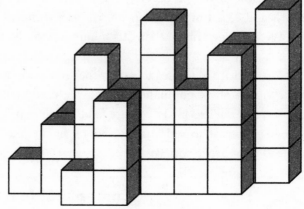

### Numerical

**2**

Continue the sequence:

$$2, \quad 3, \quad 5, \quad 10, \quad \underline{\phantom{00}}$$

### Logical

**3**

True or false:

Some buttons are seagulls. Some chariots are seagulls. Some buttons are bananas. Some chariots are bananas. Therefore some bananas are seagulls.

## Verbal-Linguistic

Pick the odd-word-out:

multitudinous, variegated, dappled, polychromatic, versicolored.

There are various other aspects or 'domains' to IQ, some measurable, some not. Earl Hunt, in his essay "The Role of Intelligence in Modern Society" sees intelligence as a conceptual variable and points out that the way intelligence is measured — the operational definition of that intelligence, will affect the results achieved.

Other variables involved in measuring intellect mean that it is impossible to pin an individual down to an IQ score with any degree of certainty. From day to day in comparable tests, the same person may have a measured variance of as much as thirty IQ points. Among the things that may affect your score are emotional well being (the happier you are the higher your score is likely to be within your own personal limits); circadian rhythms (sleep patterns); blood sugar levels (dependent upon the food you eat); physical fitness (studies in Manchester University have shown that the same person can score twenty points more in a comparable IQ test just by getting fit); test sophistication (the more you practice IQ tests, the better you are likely to score); and personal expectations (positive thinkers who expect to do well are likely to do better than negative thinkers who expect to fail). There are many other factors involved. Our ability to think clearly is easily affected by illness or its after-effects. It would also be foolish to take an IQ test when tired, or with Valium or marijuana or alcohol in your blood. Thus, to achieve the optimum score, it helps to do some thinking ahead.

## Motivation

A high IQ is an asset in this world, but it is only one aspect of personality, and it is often the least important aspect. Studies within Mensa and elsewhere have shown that people of high intelligence tend to be more conventionally successful than people of lower intelligence, and it has been shown that IQ and earning capacity are directly related, but not everyone who has a high IQ chooses to go down that route. You may choose not to plan your time, preferring a leisurely or disorganized existence. Success means different things to different people and to those of high intelligence and sensitivity, the quiet life can be seen as having greater value than material success. Desire for personal achievement in conventional terms has to be measured against the value of peace of mind, more unplanned free time, better family life, and perhaps, escape from the rat race. High IQ thus brings the freedom to choose in the same way that money brings freedom.

On the other hand, many people with relatively low IQ scores achieve a great deal in this world. Most people have some idea of their own limitations and will compensate for those limitations by working harder. In school and college, given an intellectually gifted student who is not motivated to work and a student with an average IQ who has a high degree of motivation, the average student will usually achieve the best results. Albert Einstein, despite having an IQ of around 169, initially failed the entrance exam for Zurich Polytechnic. Fortunately for Einstein, and for the world, he had the motivation to work at the things he enjoyed and 14 years later he became a professor at the same university.

Stories of success after failure are common among the highly intelligent. W.C. Fields, the sharp-witted comedian, lost his lifetime's savings after the age of 60. Instead of giving in to despair, he used his fluid intelligence and applied his talents to a new area — the emerging moving picture industry. He soon regained his fortune. Thomas Edison tried many thousands of combinations before he managed to get a working light bulb that was reliable. John Creasey had over 600 rejections before he got his first book published . . . If you are smart enough you will eventually learn what to do to achieve the success you desire.

We often find that when a person applies effort in the area which they enjoy most, they excel. But when they apply their efforts unwisely, they fail. Epicurus (300BC), put this best when he said,

*"Every man should examine his own genius, and consider what is proper to apply himself to; for nothing can be more distant from tranquility and happiness than to be engaged in a course of life for which nature has rendered us unfit.*
*An active life is not to be undertaken by an inactive person, nor an inactive life by an active person; to one, rest is quiet and action labor; to another, rest is labor and action quiet.*
*A gentle man should avoid a military life, a bold and impatient man the easy; for one cannot brook war, nor the other peace."*

# Test your personal motivation by completing the following quiz:

|  | A | B | C |
|---|---|---|---|
| *I believe this: 4 points* | | | |
| *Sometimes: 2 points* | | | |
| *Not true: 0 points* | | | |
| I am a self-made person. | X | | |
| I am a good time-keeper. | | | X |
| My work is very important to me. | X | | |
| I plan my way ahead and follow the plan. | | | X |
| I read motivational literature. | X | | |
| I believe in positive thinking. | | | X |
| I compete to beat others. | | | X |
| I feel superior to other people. | | X | |
| I make decisions quickly and stick to them. | | X | |
| I keep a tidy workspace. | | | X |
| Other people look up to me. | X | | |
| I never get despondent. | X | | |
| I keep myself fit. | X | | |
| I am ambitious. | | X | |
| I make my own luck. | X | | |
| I complete tasks that I begin. | | | X |
| I rarely procrastinate. | | X | |
| I know what I want and I get it. | | X | |
| I use my good ideas. | | X | |
| I feel very self-assured. | X | | |
| *Column Totals* | | 12 | 24 |
| *Score = A+B+C* | | 3 6 | |

**Scoring: 80-60 points**
Excellent. You have very high motivation and will undoubtedly succeed.

**40-58 points**
Very good. You are likely to do well in life.

**20-38 points**
You have some motivation, but need to think more positively.

**00-20 points**
You are not interested in success. Relax and have a great life.

# The Drawbacks of High Intelligence

High intelligence can actually be a handicap. Clever students may be bored by the lessons and spend their time daydreaming or being disruptive. Einstein's teacher of Greek once told him, "You will never amount to anything." Einstein was a teacher's worst nightmare — he asked questions which they could not answer. Although he has claimed to be a "poor student", in fact he was top of the class in subjects which interested him. What really bored Einstein were dull uninspiring lessons, and he says, "I preferred . . . to endure all sorts of punishments rather than learn to gabble by rote."

He became so disruptive that at the age of fifteen, he was asked to leave Luitpold Gymnasium, being told that his mere presence spoiled the respect of the rest of the class for the teacher.

Faced with a child of high intelligence, parents and teachers can feel inadequate and may try to redress the balance by unconsciously bringing the child back down to a subordinate position. The cure for this problem is to be aware of it. Too many gifted children still go through school with their abilities unrecognized and may give little or no indication of their giftedness. They may even give a negative indication and have learning difficulties caused, among other things, by an inability to apply themselves to work which they find boring. It can take a lot of effort to constantly stimulate the mind of a gifted child.

High IQ children often suffer from their peers too. Nobody likes to be made to feel inferior, and children can be particularly cruel in their attempts to redress the balance. Physical and mental bullying can destroy the sensitive ego of an intellectually gifted child. With this in mind the Mensa Foundation for Gifted Children (MFGC) and other such organizations do valuable work in teacher training and in assessment, counselling and support of gifted children.

A high IQ can also be a drawback in the workplace. Employers may fear to take on anybody more intelligent than themselves in the same way that Napoleon would allow nobody taller than himself in his presence. A survey of a hundred companies recently showed that it is best not to mention membership of a high IQ society on a job application.

Intelligent people also tend to find it more difficult to fit into a comfortable place in a less intelligent society. With an IQ of 145, you are in the top three percent of the population, which means that you may have no friends or acquaintances that can talk to you on your own level. That is not quite enough to get you into Mensa, but you are likely to be the only one in your class or on the factory floor or in the office with an IQ of that level — including the teacher or the boss. That is bound to lead to a feeling of isolation. Thus, many high IQ people have learned to hide their intelligence. Students may deliberately give wrong answers in order to fit in with a class of lower intelligence. Adults may pretend to be amused by the crude jokes and prejudices of their workmates. Anything to conform.

In the words of Cecilia Francesca de Arrom, who wrote as Caballero, "Intelligence is a luxury, sometimes useless, sometimes fatal. It is a torch or firebrand according to the use one makes of it."

Fortunately the compensations of having a high IQ usually make up for the drawbacks. Intelligent people get more out of life. They have more insight into the world around us and are less likely to make the sort of mistakes which ruin lives. Hence, if they come to terms with their intelligence and find some form of intellectual release, they tend to live happier and more productive lives than their less intelligent counterparts. A 45-year study of 1000 high IQ children in California by Professor Lewis Madison Terman showed that compared to a control group they did better in every way. They earned more, had better standards of living, were less likely to turn to crime, and even had more stable relationships.

# Social intelligence

Intelligence is not, of course, necessary for happiness. Even with a low psychometric IQ, If you are good at getting on with people, you are likely to be more content than someone who has a higher IQ but is no good at relationships. This is social intelligence, or SI, and it can be a very useful asset. Life is a relationship continuum and thinking skills go far beyond the ability to do puzzles. High SI individuals can often do better in life than those who have high IQ without much SI. That said, rather too much has been made of the differences and not enough of the convergences. It has to be said that it would be unusual for very high SI to exist in a person with a low IQ, and the reverse is also true. It happens, but it is not the norm. Thus, the categorizing of high IQ individuals as cold and calculating and high SI individuals as warm and caring is a false dichotomy.

It is much more difficult to measure SI than IQ. SI tests are usually of the self-analysis type such as the previous Personal Motivation Test. The results depend on the individual being truthful. Few people will willingly admit that they are cold and calculating. We are all capable of self-deceit. How many of us would fail an exam if we were responsible for marking the exam? It is not difficult to know which answer of the choices given in an SI test would be the preferred one, just as in a Rorschach ink-blot test it would be preferable for purposes of establishing your sanity to see a butterfly sitting on a wild rose rather than a vampire bat sucking your mother's blood.

# Creative Intelligence

If you are more intelligent than average, there is a 50% chance that you will also be more creative than average. However, many creative people do not have high IQs and they still manage to achieve works of great merit. It is more difficult to measure creativity than to measure IQ. A standard test for creative intelligence would be to ask you, for example, to name twenty new uses for a pail of water. Do that now. You have 5 minutes (*write your results on the table overleaf*):

## The Bucket Test

1 .........................................................................................................................
2 .........................................................................................................................
3 .........................................................................................................................
4 .........................................................................................................................
5 .........................................................................................................................
6 .........................................................................................................................
7 .........................................................................................................................
8 .........................................................................................................................
9 .........................................................................................................................
10 .......................................................................................................................
11 .......................................................................................................................
12 .......................................................................................................................
13 .......................................................................................................................
14 .......................................................................................................................
15 .......................................................................................................................
16 .......................................................................................................................
17 .......................................................................................................................
18 .......................................................................................................................
19 .......................................................................................................................
20 .......................................................................................................................

## Scoring The Bucket Test

Your thinking may be unique and highly creative, or mundane and easily thought of, and your creativity is likely to be proportional to the unique, useful and creative nature of your answers. In particular the usefulness of your answers can indicate whether your unique thought processes are the result of rational or irrational thought. Sociopaths may have unique uses for a bucket of water, but those uses are likely to involve drowning animals, committing suicide or murder, gaining revenge on those whom they feel have done them an injustice, and torture. If your answers are like that, get help!

Those who are creative but more rational are more likely to think up funny uses, or uses that could be of benefit to society as a whole, such as to pour over someone who is suffering from sunstroke, to cool the feet of those who failed at a firewalking ceremony, to use as the pendulum on a large clock, to throw over a streaker who was disrupting a game of football.

Since The Bucket Test is an open question to which you could make any reply, it would be impossible to score your answers in any definitive way here. Get someone whose judgement you trust to score the test using the following guidelines:
**Score one point for every good original and useful answer.**

Half points, or no points for less good answers, depending on originality and usefulness.

No points for sociopathic answers.

**15-20 Points:**
You are a highly creative individual. Your creativity could make you wealthy.
**10-14 Points:**
Very good. Your creative skills will prove useful to you.
**05-09 Points:**
You have some good ideas. Don't let them go to waste.
**00-04 Points:**
Creativity is not your strong point, but you probably have many other talents.

## Creativity and Functional Disorders

There is some link between creativity, intelligence, mood disorders, and functional impairment. Dyslexia is unusually common among the creatively intelligent. It is as though the brain has compensated for having problems with reading and word recognition by overdeveloping some other areas, just as a blind person may develop extraordinarily acute hearing. Manic depressives too, may produce highly original and even brilliant work during their manic phase and discard it as useless during their depressive phase, only to return to the project during their next manic phase. Samuel Johnson did his writing during his manic phase. W. Axl Rose, the rock musician, produces frenzied violent music during his manic highs and gentle ballads during his lows.

One study of writers in the USA showed that 80% had mood disorders. A UK study shows that dysfunctionality is more common among all highly creative people than among those who are not creative. Creative people are more sensitive. Sensitive people are more self-analytical and are thus more likely to become unhappy with their lot. This in turn is likely to aggravate any potential for mood disorder which exists. Most psychotic episodes have trigger events such as failing an exam or being criticized by a loved one.

Other functional disorders like autism, do not naturally lend themselves to divergent thinking. Autistic people are constantly looking inward, absorbed in self-centered subjective thought. They are prone to daydreaming, fantasies, hallucinations and delusions, and may find it difficult to apply themselves to exterior problems unconnected with their own well-being. However, not all autistic people are of subnormal psychometric intelligence, although even highly intelligent autists can appear to be, because of their withdrawal from the surrounding world. What most autistic people lack is the ability to put their insights to use in the world, but those who do learn to focus their very high powers of concentration can achieve the extraordinary.

Autistic savants often have much lower than normal IQ levels (between 35 and 75) and yet have very high degrees of skill, usually in one specific area — such as memory, numeracy, music, or art. The best known fictional example of this was the character Dustin Hoffman played in the film *The Rain Man* — a character with quite a high degree of functionality who had both an extraordinary memory and could do instant complex mental calculations. Such savants really do exist. Stephen Wiltshire is perhaps the best known of these, with his ability to produce very detailed architectural drawings from memory. Unlike artists with normal or high creative and psychometric IQ, he is able to do this even months after looking at a building.

Contrary to popular belief, we all indulge in some degree of autistic thinking and in some cases this is when we produce our best ideas. Just before falling asleep or immediately upon waking, for example, it is common for half-remembered dream images and fantasies to merge with waking thoughts, producing highly creative results. This is when eureka experiences occur, and it is often useful to keep a notepad beside the bed to jot down ideas when they occur, before they are swept away in the river of lost dreams.

## Assertiveness

The people most likely to get on in this world are not always the most intelligent. It is often those who stand up and when the need arises, push to the front of the queue for the things they want. Being assertive doesn't necessarily mean tramping other people on the way to the front of the queue, but it does mean not getting tramped on yourself. On the other hand, if you are too aggressive you could be harming your career prospects just as much. Overbearing, domineering managers destroy the morale of the workforce. The best type of manager is assertive without being a bully, and sensitive to the needs of the workforce, without being a pushover.

Complete the following quiz to find out just how assertive you are, and in the process you'll discover a lot more about who you really are, and what motivates you. Be honest with yourself; self-knowledge can only come through honesty.

## Assertiveness Quiz

Tick in the one box that most closely describes how you think you would react:

**1) You discover that a colleague has taken credit for some of your work. Do you:**
☒ (a) Tell your boss and insist that the colleague is reprimanded
☐ (b) Keep it to yourself, but never again trust the colleague
☐ (c) Insist that the colleague goes to your boss and explains what happened

**2) While checking accounts you realize that you have made a serious mistake that has cost your firm money. Do you:**

☐ (a) Arrange things so that someone else gets the blame

☐ (b) Hide the mistake at all costs

☒ (c) Admit the mistake and show how it could be avoided in future

**3) Your boss refuses to give you time off that you need. Do you:**

☒ (a) Threaten to quit unless you get the time off, or call in sick and take the time off anyway

☐ (b) Realize that you probably don't deserve the time off, and accept the decision with disappointment

☐ (c) Point out the value of your contribution to the firm, and offer to work extra hours to cover for the time off

**4) You have just been awarded a large bonus for a major success at work. Do you:**

☒ (a) Make sure everyone knows that it was all your own work

☐ (b) Get all embarrassed and try to ensure that nobody finds out

☐ (c) Hold a party and acknowledge that you couldn't have done it without the contribution of others

**5) After making a major decision, you realize that it was wrong. Do you:**

☒ (a) Stick to your decision, because to change your mind would show weakness

☐ (b) Realize that you are a fool, and that you'll never be much good at decisions, then change your mind

☐ (c) Reassess the situation and make another decision, in the knowledge that we all make mistakes

**6) A friend comes to you with a problem, asking for help. Do you:**

☐ (a) Tell the friend that you have your own problems to deal with, and have no time for theirs

☒ (b) Take the problem in hand and solve it yourself

☐ (c) Help if you can, without feeling obliged to

**7) You don't understand what you are being asked to do. Do you:**

☒ (a) Take your best shot, and hope to bluff your way through

☐ (b) Secretly ask a friend for help later

☐ (c) Immediately ask for more information, even if everyone else understands

**8) Someone is cruel to you. Do you:**

☒ (a) Take immediate revenge

☐ (b) Shrink into your shell, hurt

☐ (c) Confront the person, and tell them how you feel about what they did

**9) Your boss, whom you do not find attractive, makes sexual advances to you. Do you:**

- ☒ (a) Slap him/her on the face, and storm out, before claiming constructive dismissal
- ☐ (b) Submit, in the knowledge that your job will be safeguarded
- ☐ (c) Politely reject the advance, and explain that you never mix business and pleasure

**10) A person whom you know to be a fool gives you a piece of advice. Do you:**

- ☐ (a) Ignore the advice
- ☐ (b) Take the advice, because the fool probably knows better than you
- ☒ (c) Consider the advice, and take it if you find it to be sound, even if everyone else laughs

*In the following questions, tick the box that most closely describes the way you feel about yourself:*

**11) About your self-image, would you say:**

- ☐ (a) "I am better than anyone else"
- ☒ (b) "Most others are better than me"
- ☐ (c) "I am as good as anyone else"

**12) About your decisions, would you say:**

- ☐ (a) "I am always right"
- ☐ (b) "I am usually wrong"
- ☒ (c) "I am usually right, but I do make mistakes"

**13) About your friends, would you say:**

- ☒ (a) "I don't need friends"
- ☐ (b) "I don't have many friends because I'm careful whom I mix with"
- ☐ (c) "I have lots of friends and make new friends easily"

**14) About your personal responsibility, would you say:**

- ☐ (a) "I seek out responsibility"
- ☒ (b) "I dislike responsibility"
- ☐ (c) "I accept responsibility when I need to"

**15) About your self-confidence, would you say:**

- ☐ (a) "I am supremely confident"
- ☒ (b) "I lack confidence"
- ☐ (c) "I am naturally confident"

**16) About your temper, would you say:**

- ☐ (a) "I tend to fly off the handle a lot"
- ☒ (b) "I suppress my anger, but get emotionally upset"
- ☐ (c) "I express anger, but never let it get out of hand"

**17) About your beliefs, would you say:**

- ☒ (a) "I am dogmatic, because my beliefs are the right ones"
- ☐ (b) "I'm not quite sure what I believe, because I've never thought about it"
- ☐ (c) "I have come to a set of beliefs through my experience, but would be willing to change in the light of new knowledge"

**18) About your ambitions, would you say:**

☐ (a) "I am ruthlessly ambitious"

☒ (b) "I don't really have ambitions"

☐ (c) "I am working towards the achievement of my ambitions"

**19) About your ability to relax, would you say:**

☐ (a) "I rarely relax; I just don't have time"

☐ (b) "I can't relax; there is always something grinding on my nerves"

☒ (c) "I take time to relax because I feel that's importan"

**20) About your response to criticism, would you say:**

☒ (a) "I hate being criticized, and react to it badly"

☐ (b) "I feel that I need criticism. I do a lot that deserves it"

☐ (c) "I listen to criticism and learn from it"

## In the following questions, tick the box that is closest to the truth about the way you feel or react:

**21) About stress, would you say :**

☒ (a) "I get very stressed up by some situations."

☐ (b) "I just can't cope with stress, so I avoid it."

☐ (c) "I cope well with stress. I use it to keep me on top."

**22) About doing things:**

☐ (a) "Just to be awkward, I refuse to do things that people want me to do."

☒ (b) "I just can't seem to say no when others want me to do things."

☐ (c) "If I don't want to do something, I politely refuse to do it, because my wants are important."

**23) About arguments:**

☒ (a) "I never lose an argument, because I don't give in."

☐ (b) "I can't argue with people. It is a waste of time even trying, because I always lose."

☐ (c) "I state my case, but when someone can't see my point of view I don't argue after letting them know what I feel."

**24) About trust:**

☐ (a) "I don't trust others, and they don't trust me."

☒ (b) "I'd like other people to trust me, but rarely seem to get that trust. I tend to give my trust to those who break it."

☐ (c) "I enjoy the trust of others, and those I give my trust to rarely break it."

**25) About flattery:**

☐ (a) "I like to have people around who will flatter me."

☒ (b) "I suspect that when people flatter me, they are being dishonest."

☐ (c) "I can accept honest flattery, because I have worth, but I discourage crawlers."

**26 About team-sports:**
☐ (a) "I enjoy team-sports, but I get angry when other players can't keep up with me, or when they make mistakes."
☐ (b) "I dislike team-sports, and I'm not very good at them."
☒ (c) "I enjoy team-sports, and I'm good at them."

**27) At meetings:**
☐ (a) "I make sure that everyone hears what I have to say, whether they want to or not."
☐ (b) "I'm nervous about speaking out in front of others, so I tend to hide in a corner."
☒ (c) "I speak up when I have a valid point to make."

**28) About approval:**
☐ (a) "I neither want nor need the approval of others."
☒ (b) "I have a need for the approval of others."
☐ (c) "I don't need the approval of others for what I do, but when I get it I'm happy."

**29) About truth:**
☐ (a) "I tell people what I think even if it hurts them."
☒ (b) "I tell lies to avoid unpleasant situations."
☐ (c) "I generally speak the truth, but I'll tell a lie to avoid hurting others."

**30) About physical control:**
☒ (a) "I've been known to lash out in anger, but I'm always sorry afterwards."
☐ (b) "I've never had the urge to lash out."
☐ (c) "I've sometimes felt like lashing out, but I always restrain myself."

## Scoring the Assertiveness Quiz

The greatest value in this type of quiz is what you learn about yourself in the process of completing it. The following comments are for guidance, but where they stray from what you feel to be true, go with your instincts. If you score close to a borderline, read the next comments too.

## Score mostly Cs:

You are assertive, but not to the point of being overbearing. You are cool, controlled and confident, with just the right amount of consideration for others. You have a very high degree of social intelligence. You are fully aware of your right to have and assert your own needs, and to express your feelings, and with your excellent judgement of human nature you can see when others lack your qualities. You are helpful to others, but if you don't want to do something you know that you have the right to refuse, and you don't get embarrassed at saying no. Because you know how to be diplomatic you usually get what you want. With your high intelligence, your confidence in your own abilities, and your top people-management skills you deserve to be in a good management position. Don't let your talents go to waste.

## Score mostly Bs:

You have many wonderful qualities, such as kindness, compassion, and sensitivity, but you are too considerate for your own good. You are trying too hard to fit in. People are bound to take advantage of you if you behave like a human door-mat. You are also a timebomb of suppressed emotions. You may get tension headaches and other psychosomatic problems. Your career is unlikely to be progressing much — if you get promoted it will be because someone has died or left. To change things you need to become more assertive. Learn to say what you think. Don't be afraid to express your emotions, and don't be so afraid of what others think. You don't have to give up caring for others to have your own wants and needs fulfilled. Your place in this world is just as important as anyone else's.

## Score mostly As:

You are assertive to the point of being a bully. This doesn't mean that you are necessarily a bad person, but you have got into a system of thinking, and a pattern of life that is non-beneficial. You are likely to have very high psychometric IQ, but by your aggressiveness you alienate people, and instead of getting more co-operation out of them you get less. You probably lack genuine confidence, and cover that up with bluster and brashness. You will have few if any genuine friends, although you may, if you are in a senior position at work have a number of 'hangers on' who pretend to like you because they are scared of you. Your social life is likely to be non-existent, unless you go out on your own, and you may be very unhappy with your present life.

The way to change is to start recognizing the rights of others. What you need is important, but what other people need is important too. To have a friend you need to be a friend. Everyone has the right to be treated with respect, and even if you are superior to them in rank or position, you have no right to bully them. Gradually, you will find that when you give people respect, and take their wants and needs into account, you will receive respect and generosity in return, and your currently low self-esteem will be replaced by a new feeling of personal worth.

## Male-female differences

On average, men have brains which are slightly larger than the brains of women, but the difference is probably because men, on the whole, are bigger than women. There is no overall IQ differential between men and women. Men are better at spatial and related problems; women are better at verbal-linguistic problems. Interestingly there is a large hormonal component to the differential. During menstruation, when women have low estrogen levels, their spatial cognitive powers can double. They are also more likely to be assertive at this time. Men do best at verbal problems when their testosterone levels are lowest, but are less likely to be assertive at this time. Girls who have been subjected to high levels of testosterone in the womb develop unusually high visual-spatial abilities and other masculine traits.

There are other forces at work here too. Although girls tend to apply themselves more to schoolwork, research has shown that girls taught in an all-girl class do better in related subjects such as science, technical drawing, and maths, than they would if taught in a mixed class. When there are boys present the boys tend to be more pushy than girls and thus attract more of the teacher's time. Thus, although girls are working harder and should do better, they are receiving less teaching time and so do worse. Teachers can do a lot to help balance the books in this area by ensuring that they divide their time equally.

# Artificial intelligence

Computers are currently doubling in power every eighteen months and we now have computers which can recognize voices and respond to commands. They have "learned" to react to light and darkness, recognize shapes, communicate with us and with each other, and in some cases, self-repair.

Computers can even write poetry, and recently the first novel by a computer has been published, but this does not mean that computers can think. Not yet anyway. The poetry is not very good, and the novel was not very literate.

Probably the area where computers have the greatest 'thinking' success is in chess, but even here we are at a very early stage of development. It took a great deal of human input for IBM's Deep Blue computer to recently beat World Chess Champion Gary Kasparov. And in the sense of humor department, not normally Kasparov's greatest strength, he beat the computer hands down.

Long before Kasparov's encounter with Deep Blue, the British computer scientist Alan Turing looked at the question of whether machines can think and proposed a test of computer IQ which has now been dubbed the Turing test. Turing's test was simple — If you can be fooled by the computer into thinking it is a person, (by communicating through a phone or a keyboard) the computer can be said to think. So far, no computer has ever passed the Turing test when faced with the penetrating questions of an inquisitive human. When a sentence structure that the computer is incapable of answering comes along, computers are programmed to respond by incorporating that word structure or meaning into the answer. For example, if you were to ask the computer, "Tell me why it is better to fall in love than to eat a shrimp," the computer may answer, "Why do you ask me such a foolish question about love and shrimps?"

A human respondent, on the other hand, would be more likely to say, "Love is food for the soul, but a shrimp is food only for the body."

How long will it be before a computer can compare with the wit of Voltaire, who, when told that life is hard, asked, "Compared to what?"

Initially a correspondent may be fooled by the computer's answer, but a number of abstract questions or statements are likely to reveal the computer's lack of thinking depth to a respondent with good human IQ. That said, less intelligent respondents are likely to be fooled by the computer, and with greater computer power and more complex algorithms, the time will come when the average desktop computer will be able to pass the Turing test with ease.

# Critical Thinking

In this modern age we are exposed to a great deal of information from many sources and it is not always easy to judge the accuracy of the information that comes our way. The following nine steps form a good framework for judgement of the accuracy of any argument. Ask yourself the following:

1. What are the problems addressed and the conclusions reached?

2. What is the justification for reaching these conclusions?

3. Are the originator's conclusions logical and valid?

4. What errors in reasoning have been made by the originator?

5. Which words or phrases are ambiguous?

6. Have assumptions have been made, and if so, are they based on logic?

7. Has the originator used relevant analogies or metaphors?

8. Could entirely different conclusions have been consistent with the facts?

9. Are there rival hypotheses to those which the originator uses?

A good IQ does not necessarily make you a clear thinker, it merely indicates that you have the potential to be so. Many mistakes are possible, even for the intellectually gifted. Some of the mistakes are obvious, others less so. Thinking accurately is a skill that needs to be learned like any other skill

To quote Shakespeare,

*"Thoughts are but dreams till their effects be tried."*

# Here are some of the most common errors of thinking and their cures:

| Error | Details or Example | Workaround |
|---|---|---|
| Using a non sequitur | Reasoning that does not follow logically from anything previously said | Critically examine all conclusions to see if they are logical |
| Plunging in | Gathering information and reaching conclusions too soon | Ensure that you know what the real problem is that you have to solve |
| Jumping to conclusions | Guessing the answer to a problem rather than solving the problem | Collect key factual information and use that to solve problems |
| Failure to distinguish between fact and opinion | Believing rumor to be true. Relying on anecdotal evidence | Check the truth of statements before believing them |
| Lack of problem definition | Failing to consciously define the problem or being unduly influenced by the definitions of others | Examine what is actually happening. Define problems from your own evidence |
| Not using the all facts | Lack of research or selection of facts which fit your preconceptions. | Find out all the facts and base your decisions upon them |
| Prejudice | The inclination to take a stand with insufficient information | Never prejudge people or situations. Do not defend or attack without good reason |
| Self-deceit | Failing to understand your own limitations. Believing that you are more able than you are | Acquiring self-knowledge |
| Lack of discrimination | Failing to weigh the facts according to importance. Believing that all propositions are equally valid | Careful consideration of what matters and what does not matter |
| Filling a personal need | Embracing arguments that meet your personal requirements | Detach yourself from the argument. |
| Over-simplification | Ignoring the middle ground in a controversy | Embrace complexity and organize and consider all the facts |
| False syllogism | All ducks have feathers. All birds have feathers. Therefore all birds are ducks | Because D has f and B has f does not make B = D. Other things may also have f |
| Circular argument | I know that this book is true because this is a book which is known to be true | Seek empirical evidence of the truth |
| Closed thinking | What is the point of investigating this when I already know the truth? | Keep an open mind. You may hold wrong opinions |

## Organized Thinking

Few people have a clear idea of what they want from life. It is ironic that we are likely to spend more time planning our annual vacation than planning our lives. We tend to let life happen and when it does it takes us by surprise. Planning is one of those things we approve of, but rarely indulge in, but it is fundamental to the process of problem solving. Whatever your problem, you have to plan how to solve it, and most situations in life can be viewed as problems to be solved. If you want to pass an exam, the problem is *how can I ensure that I pass this exam?* . . . . Those who plan study periods into their schedule achieve more success in exams. If you want a successful career, the problem is *how can I have a successful career?* . . . Those who plan their career achieve more promotion and job success.

It all boils down to planning our time. Those who plan their time achieve more of everything.

> *"There is nothing of which we are apt to be so lavish as of time, and about which we ought to be more solicitous; since without it we can do nothing in this world. Time is what we want most, but alas! we use worst. . ."*
>
> William Penn

William Penn's famous book *Some Fruits of Solitude,* was written, like a number of his works, while he was in prison for expressing his political and religious beliefs. Like Voltaire, who started *Henriade* in prison — the poem that made him famous, and Aleksandr Solzhenitsyn, who wrote and memorized *One Day in the Life of Ivan Denisovitch* while in a labor camp, and John Bunyan, who began *Pilgrim's Progress* in prison, Penn made good use of his time in prison rather than waste it. Better use, no doubt, than most who were free. Thus he became an inspiring leader to many.

Deep down, despite the tendency to deceive ourselves, we all know that we waste too much time. No matter what our IQ, we all procrastinate. We let our dreams trickle down the TV tube. We never get round to taking that cruise, or learning that language, or building that boat. Our best days slip away like shadows, while we idly watch them pass.

Asked to instantly choose between 2,700; 27,000; 270,000; and 27,000,000 as the number of days in the average life, (choose now!) most people are overoptimistic by at least a factor of 10. In fact, based on a lifetime of 73 years, we have less than 27,000 days to live. It doesn't seem much because it is not much. We may, of course, have more, but we may have much less, and a lot of us will already be more than halfway there. The truth is that we have no way of knowing what the future holds. We can rely only on the time we have right now.

Isaac Pitman, inventor of the shorthand system of writing, said, "Well-arranged time is the surest mark of a well-arranged mind," and that seems to be true in every case, just as the converse is true. In fact, since we think sequentially, our thoughts are organized in time sequence, so by organizing our time we organize the way we think, and this in turn can improve our creativity and boost our performance in every area, affecting both our psychometric IQ score and our ability to make use of that intelligence in the real world.

In business especially, using our time to the fullest can pay great dividends. Since most people waste hours of every working day, those who really make use of their time can achieve more — sometimes so much more that others are astonished. That is why, if you want something done, it is usually better to ask a busy person. However, there are many ways of being busy. Disorganized people can be twice as busy achieving nothing as organized people are getting things done. In the words of Benjamin Franklin, "He who does everything, does nothing."

# 17 Steps to Organized Thinking

## 1. Plan each day the night before.

Write the things you need to do on separate cards and stack them in order of priority. The following day, start with the top card and tackle them one at a time until they have all been completed. Keep a few blank cards for the unexpected. (Ordinary business cards are great for the purpose and are very inexpensive when blank. Plus, they are easy to slip into your purse or pocket.)

## 2. Use the do-it-now system.

Don't keep a pending tray, either mentally, or actually. Deal with paper the first time it is read. This is the most valuable of all time-savers, and since the only way the do-it-now system can be implemented is to become an instant decision maker, it can transform your life on the spot. But it means no more put-off letters and phone calls.

## 3. Speed-read.

The simple action of trying to read faster can double the average reading speed. Get into the **SEE** mode - **S**can for **E**ssential **E**lements. Practice the **IJMBT** - **I**nstant **J**unk **M**ail **B**in **T**rick.

## 4. Always do what you say you will do.

If you don't, your valuable time will be wasted by people chasing you up to find out why things haven't been done. Putting them off just wastes more time, because they'll get back to you again and again. Don't make promises unless you intend to keep them. Don't fail to keep them when you do make them.

## 5. Be concise.

Write memos instead of letters. Most letters can boil down to two words: *Well done; Try harder; Good luck; Hard luck; Thank you; See me.*

## 6. Delegate willingly.

Don't believe that you're the only one that can do a task. If that were true, promotion would be impossible. Delegation also helps to make other people feel important and to upgrade their skills. It is also good planning. The more you delegate, the more you'll be able to delegate in future, and the more time you'll have free.

## 7. Stay focussed.

Loss of mental focus accounts for almost a third of the time taken for tasks. With focussed attention therefore, a third as much again can be achieved each day. Repeat the words 'stay focussed' whenever you feel a lapse coming on. It'll soon become a habit that saves you hours.

## 8. Solve problems immediately.

They will arise, so don't let them accumulate. It also makes sense not to cause them in the first place. Never argue. Arguing is time-wasting. If you have the power, make decisions and stick to them. If you don't have that power, compromise with good grace as soon as you can.

## 9. Cancel unnecessary meetings.

That means most meetings. Remember that people make more effective decisions when they are alone, and that includes you. If you do have to attend meetings, keep them as short as possible. People use meetings as excuses not to get work done.

## 10. Limit time on phone calls.

Before you make calls, jot down the subjects you have to deal with. On the phone go through them as fast as possible, then make excuses and hang up. If you are expecting a call from someone else, again have a list of topics pre-prepared. This is a useful technique even on personal calls.

### 11.  Set tight deadlines for yourself and others.

Deadlines force people to perform at peak. When you set the deadlines, listen carefully to the response. 'Perhaps,' usually means 'No,' and, 'I'll try,' usually means 'I won't.' Extract certainty from those you deal with instead of uncertainty. Then, you'll be able to mark the deadline in your calendar and plan ahead.

### 12.  Keep a tidy desk.

A cluttered workspace wastes time. You can't be efficient if you spend half your time chasing lost paper. Worse still, if you keep a cluttered desk and you are the boss, other people will emulate your inefficiency, with a resultant effect on your business. If necessary go in at the weekend to clear the desk. With the do-it-now system, if something doesn't go into the out tray, it goes into the wastepaper basket. But don't ever throw out something you haven't yet dealt with. It'll come back to haunt you.

### 13.  Plan ahead.

If you try to run a business, or even a holiday without planning, it is like trying to cook a meal without ingredients. Diary spaces mean wasted time unless you know in advance what you'll be doing during those times. Plan to use the free periods profitably.

### 14.  Concentrate on the small things.

Save five minutes here, five minutes there, and it all adds up. Get up five minutes earlier. Spend five minutes less in the toilet. Take five minutes less coffee-break. Time yourself on the things you need to get done and do them faster each time.

### 15.  Don't say yes when you mean no.

If you take more work than you can handle, you'll regret it later and have to deal with the problems it causes you.

### 16.  Never make the same mistake twice.

Nothing wastes time like mistakes. We profit from them the first time they happen, because we learn. But the next time they happen, we lose time, energy, and profit.

## 17.  Don't ever take work home.

To do so is an admission of inefficiency at work. Tackle the inefficiency instead. The freed 'home-work' time can be used for far more important things. What, after all, is the point in saving time if we are so busy running around saving it that there is no time left for the good things in life?

With just a little bit of thought, it is possible to also greatly improve our personal lives by organizing time — surely an equally good way to use our intellect. We can plan breakfast in bed, or romantic evenings. We can plan quality time with the children, or weekends away that would be impossible without thinking ahead. Each important minute, of each and every day, we have the ultimate choice that makes anything and everything possible: what to do next. Choose wisely. Then, no matter what your IQ, it is possible to achieve a great deal.

 37,    20 (2 + 3 + 5 + 10)    False    Multitudinous

# Taking The Tests

On the following pages you'll find tests that will help you discover what your cognitive strengths and weaknesses are (they will not, however, result in a conventional IQ score). When you take them, try to simulate actual test conditions: set aside a time when you will not be interrupted, time yourself, and try to work calmly and efficiently.  Should you ever wish to take a real IQ test, these practice tests will help you to be well prepared.

A time limit of 45 minutes is allowed for each of the 14 tests.

| Score | Rating |
|-------|--------|
| 0-4 | Poor |
| 5-9 | Below average |
| 10-14 | Average |
| 15-19 | Good |
| 20-23 | Very good |
| 24-26 | Excellent |
| 27-30 | Exceptional |

### Bonanza Puzzle

A time limit of 1 hour and 15 minutes (75 minutes) is allowed for this test.

| Score | Rating |
|-------|--------|
| 0-7 | Poor |
| 8-14 | Below average |
| 15-24 | Average |
| 25-32 | Good |
| 33-40 | Very Good |
| 41-45 | Excellent |
| 46-50 | Exceptional |

## 1

Find the starting point and move from square to adjoining square, horizontally or vertically, but not diagonally, to spell a 12-letter word, using each letter once only. What are the missing letters?

| E | V | I |
|---|---|---|
| R | B | A |
| A | B | T |
| N | O | I |

## 2

Find two words with different spellings, but sound alike, that can mean:

**FROLIC / CHANCE**

## 3

What number should replace the question mark?

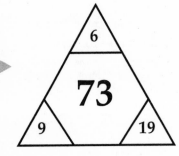 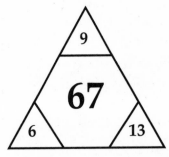 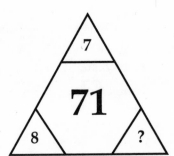

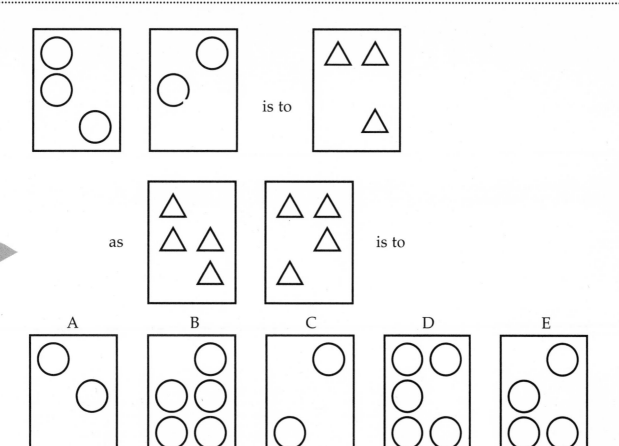

**4**

is to

as

is to

| A | B | C | D | E |

**482 : 34**

Which two numbers below have the same relationship as the two above?

**5**

A. 218 : 24
B. 946 : 42
C. 687 : 62
D. 299 : 26
E. 749 : 67

GIBE is to TAUNT as BADINAGE is to:

**6**

A. PRANK
B. REPARTEE
C. PLEASANTRY
D. WITTICISM
E. JOKE

**7**

Which of the following is the odd one out?

A. CUBE
B. SQUARE
C. SPHERE
D. CYLINDER
E. OCTAHEDRON

**8**

If you divide 552 by ¼, and then divide the result by half the original figure, what is the answer?

**9**

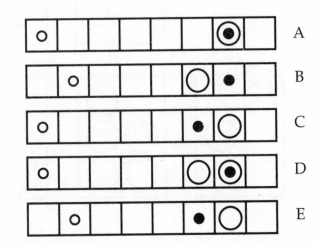

What figure to the right will continue the above sequence?

**10**

What word is opposite in meaning to EVASIVE?

A. ZEALOUS
B. EXACT
C. OPEN
D. CAUSTIC
E. BRAVE

**11**

What number should replace the question mark below?

| 6 | 3 | 4 | 6 |
|---|---|---|---|
| 5 | 5 | 7 | 4 |
| 8 | 3 | 4 | 8 |
| 3 | 9 | 7 | ? |

## 12

**PLEAD    LABEL    ALBUM    LUSTY?**

What word continues the above sequence?

       A. FROWN
       B. UTTER
       C. LUNCH
       D. DREAM
       E. CHARM

## 13

What is the answer if, from the number below, you multiply by five the number of even numbers that are immediately followed by an odd number?

4 7 8 5 3 1 9 7 8 4 4 7 8 9 2 3

## 14

Which of the five boxes below is most like the box above?

 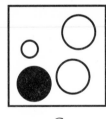  

  A         B         C         D         E

## 15

SEA PIGEON is an anagram of what nine-letter word?

Which of the following is the odd one out?

**A. SKIT**
**B. EMERITUS**
**C. LAMPOON**
**D. CLERIHEW**
**E. PARODY**

Find a six-letter word made up of only the following four letters.

**G  M**
**N  O**

What number should replace the question mark?

**34  7  29  11  23  16  16  22  ?**

A.  3
B.  5
C.  8
D. 11
E. 13

What word can be placed in front of the other five to form five new words? Each dot represents a letter.

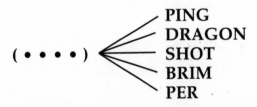

( • • • • )  PING
DRAGON
SHOT
BRIM
PER

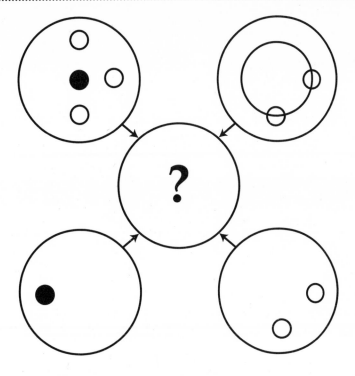

Each line and symbol that appears in the four outer circles, above, is transferred to the middle circle according to how many times it appears, as follows:

**One time — it is transferred**
**Two times — it is possibly transferred**
**Three times — it is transferred**
**Four times — it is not transferred**

Which of the circles below should appear as the middle circle?

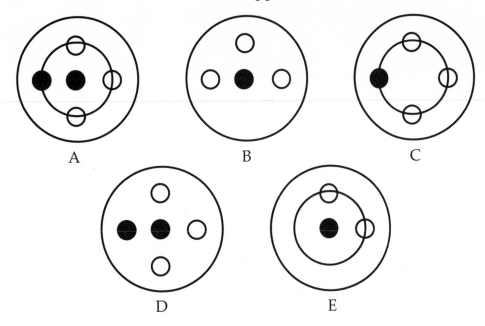

**21**

A word can be placed in the brackets that has the same meaning as the words outside. What is it?

**ENCLOSURE ( • • • • • • • • ) COMBINE**

**22**

Place two of the three-letter segments together to make a six-letter bug.

**ANT  BEE  SCA  TLY  RAB  FLY**

**23**

If the missing letters in the two circles below are correctly inserted they will form synonymous words. The words do not have to be read in a clockwise direction, but the letters are consecutive? What are the words and missing letters?

**24**

What number should replace the question mark?

A. 30
B. 32
C. 34
D. 36
E. 38

| 5 | | 4 |
|---|---|---|
| | 27 | |
| 7 | | 6 |

| 6 | | 7 |
|---|---|---|
| | 40 | |
| 9 | | 7 |

| 8 | | 4 |
|---|---|---|
| | 71 | |
| 5 | | 9 |

| 9 | | 3 |
|---|---|---|
| | ? | |
| 5 | | 4 |

42

What circle will continue the sequence and replace the question mark?

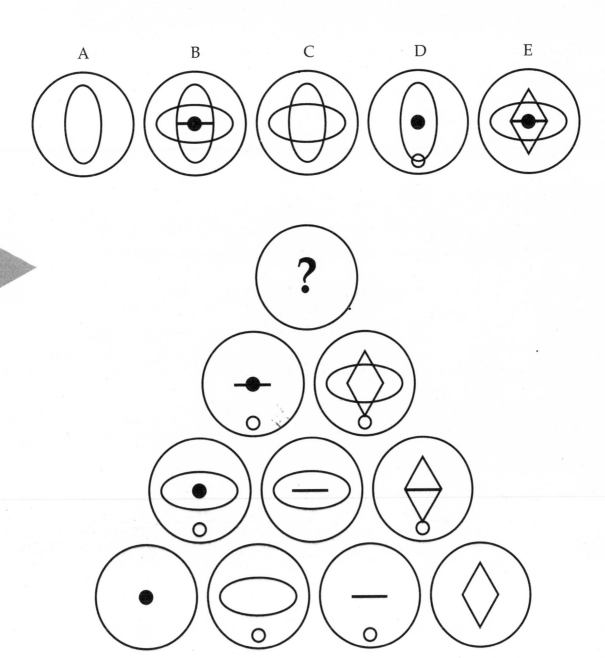

**26**

If the missing letters in the circle below are correctly inserted they will form an eight-letter word. The word will not have to be read in a clockwise direction, but the letters are consecutive. What is the word and missing letters?

**27**

Which of the following has the same meaning as MENDICANT?

**A. CHURCH OFFICIAL**
**B. REPAIRER**
**C. TEACHER**
**D. BEGGAR**
**E. CHEMIST**

**28**

CUT PERM is an anagram of what seven-letter word?

**29**

Simplify the following and find x.

$$\frac{8 \times 7}{\frac{2}{7} - \frac{2}{14}} = x$$

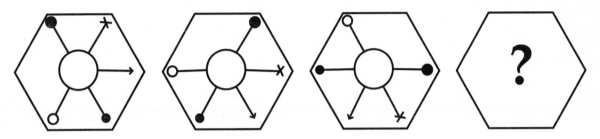

Which of A, B, C, D, or E, bottom should replace the question mark above?

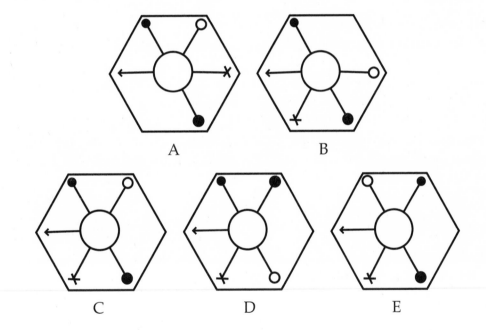

A          B

C          D          E

# Answers

**1** Abbreviation.
The missing letters are, reading from top to bottom, V, B and N.

**2** Gambol and gamble.

**3** 15.
(Top x left) + right = middle.
(7 x 8) [56] + 15 = 71.

The others are (6 x 9) [54] + 19 = 73 and (9 x 6) [54] + 13 = 67.

**4** E.
No figure in the same position in both rectangles is carried forward and figures change from triangle to circle and vice versa.

**5** B (946 : 42).
Break down left number:
(First digit x second digit) + third digit = right number.
(9 x 4) [36] + 6 = 42.
The example was (4 x 8) [32] + 2 = 34.

**6** B (Repartee).
Repartee is a synonym for badinage, as taunt is for gibe.

**7** B (Square).
The others are three-dimensional; a square is two-dimensional.

**8** 8.
552 ÷ ¼ = 2208; 2208 ÷ 276 (half of 552) = 8.

**9** A.
There are three sequences, all alternate: the small white circle moves one forward and two back; the large white circle moves one back and two forward; the small black circle moves one back and two forward.

**10** C (Open).

**11** 6.
Reading down, the sum of numbers on each row increases by two.

**12** Utter.
Each word starts with the second letter of the previous one.

**13** 25.
There are five odd numbers which follow an even one, so 5 x 5 = 25.

**14** E.
There are four circles, two black (medium-sized) and two white (one large, one small).

46

# Answers

**15** Espionage.

**16** B. Emeritus.
The others are terms of lightly poking fun.

**17** Gnomon (a pointer on a sundial).

**18** C (8).
Alternate numbers go in different sequence:
− 5, − 6, − 7, and − 8; + 4, + 5, + 6.

**19** Snap.

**20** A.

**21** Compound.

**22** Scarab.

**23** Misspend, squander. The missing letters are M and P (misspend), Q and R (squander).

**24** C (34).
The sums are (top left x bottom right) − (bottom left − top right) = middle.
(9 x 4) [36] − (5 − 3) [2] = 34.

The others are
(5 x 6) [30] − (7 − 4) [3] = 27;
(6 x 7) [42] − (9 − 7) [2] = 40;
(8 x 9) [72] − (5 − 4) [1] = 71.

**25** E.
Different symbols in adjoining circles on the same row are carried into the circle between them in the row above. Similar symbols in the same place are dropped.

**26** Henchman.
The missing letters are both H.

**27** D (beggar).

**28** Crumpet.

**29** 392. 2/14 = 1/7, so 2/7 − 1/7 = 1/7. 8 x 7 = 56. 56 ÷ 1/7 = 56 x 7/1. 56 x 7 = 392.

**30** C.
Every item rotates 60° clockwise each time.

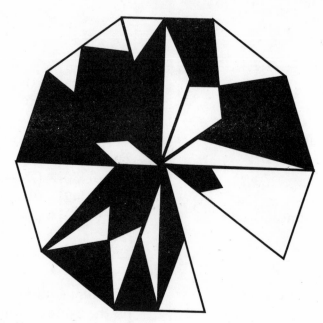

**1**

Which of the segments below is missing from the diagram above?

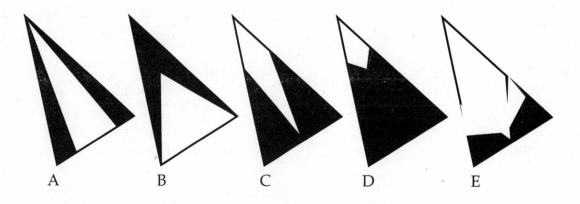

| A | B | C | D | E |

**2**

Complete the three-letter words which, reading down, will reveal a country.

T E ( • )
N I ( • )
F O ( • )
T I ( • )
B A ( • )
O B ( • )
E R ( • )

2 1 7 3 8 9 5 is to 9 7 2 5 3 8 1 as 9 6 7 4 8 1 2 is to:

A. 7 1 9 2 4 8 6
B. 7 9 1 4 2 6 8
C. 2 1 4 7 9 6 8
D. 1 7 9 2 4 8 6
E. 7 1 9 4 2 6 8

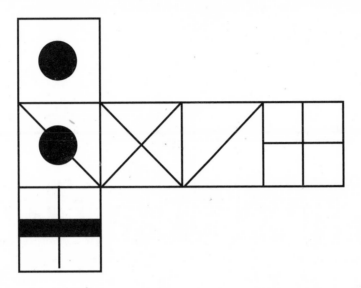

When the above is folded to form a cube, just one of the following can be produced. Which one is it?

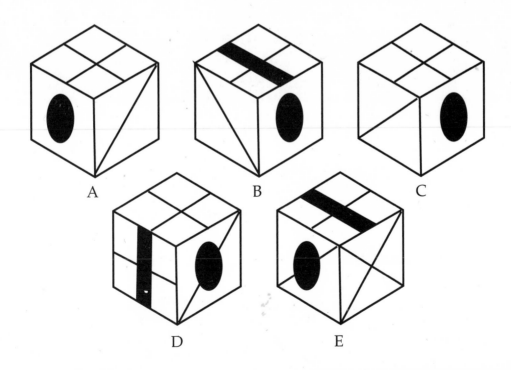

A          B          C

D          E

**5**

Which of the following is the odd one out?

> **A. MISSAL**
> **B. LEXICON**
> **C. LECTERN**
> **D. PSALTER**
> **E. THESAURUS**

**6**

What number will replace the question mark?

| | 72 | |
|---|---|---|
| 83 | 7 | 55 |
| | 37 | |

| | 19 | |
|---|---|---|
| 25 | 3 | 13 |
| | 4 | |

| | 73 | |
|---|---|---|
| 39 | ? | 3 |
| | 28 | |

**7**

Which word is a synonym of EXPRESSIVE?

> **A. PARTICULAR**
> **B. SUGGESTIVE**
> **C. POSITIVE**
> **D. INSCRUTABLE**
> **E. ELEGANT**

**8**

Complete the two words using the letters of the following once only.

**CASE A DOOR PAD**

• E • • R • T • •     • E • • R • T • •

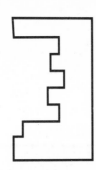

Which piece, below, can be put with the one above to form a perfect square?

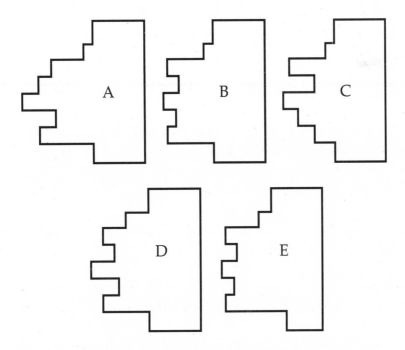

## SECOND (ARDENT) NATURE

Following the same rules as above,
what word should go in the brackets?

**VALISE ( • • • • • • ) OPENLY**

**11** What two words are opposite in meaning?

A. EXPAND
B. DELIGHT
C. UPSURGE
D. OFFEND
E. UPEND
F. EQUATE

**12** Ken is half again as old as Phil, who is half again as old as David. Their ages total 152? How old is Phil?

**DOUBT : CONVICTION**

Which two words below have the same relationship as the two words above?

A. faultless : exemplary

B. fastidious : slender

C. courage : resolution

D. instinct : constancy

E. routine : abnormal

**13**

Which of the following is the odd one out?

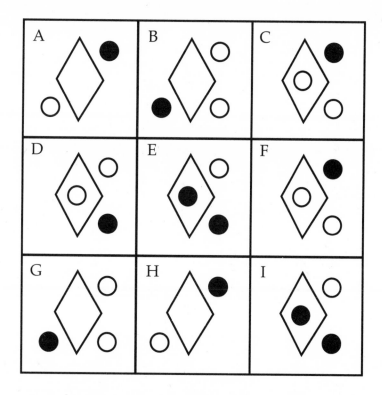

Which of the following is not an anagram of a fruit?

**A. MINK PUP**
**B. BURY REBEL**
**C. USA MAST**
**D. MANS GUT**
**E. DAMN RAIN**

What number should replace the question mark?

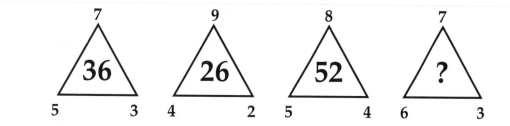

Find a six-letter word made up of only the following four letters?

L O
G I

**18**

What word can be placed in front of the other five to form five new words? Each dot represents a letter.

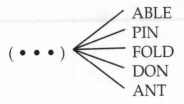

( • • • ) ⟨
ABLE
PIN
FOLD
DON
ANT

**19**

DEAD LIVER is an anagram of what nine-letter word?

**20**

Each of the nine squares in the grid marked 1A to 3C should incorporate all of the items which are shown in the squares of the same letter and number, at the left and top, respectively. For example, 2B should incorporate all of the symbols that are in squares 2 and B. One square, however, is incorrect. Which one is it?

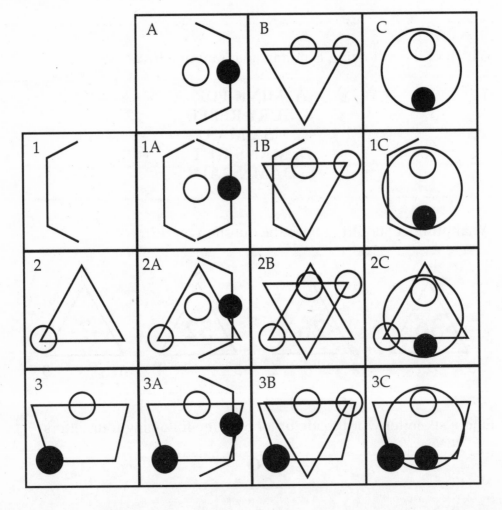

54

What word is a synonym of PAROXYSM?

A. SEIZURE
B. SUPERABUNDANCE
C. SPASMODIC
D. SPACE
E. PARODY

| 6 | 2 | 5 | 7 |
| 8 | 3 | 17 | 7 |
| 9 | 2 | 9 | 9 |
| 7 | 4 | 10 | ? |

Which of the following should replace the question mark?

A. 24
B. 30
C. 18
D. 12
E. 26

If the missing letters in the circle below are correctly inserted they will form an eight-letter word. The word will not have to be read in a clockwise direction, but the letters are consecutive. What is the word and missing letters?

A word can be placed in the brackets that has the same meaning as the words outside. What is it?

**SEARCH ( • • • • • • ) POLECAT**

Which of the following is the odd one out?

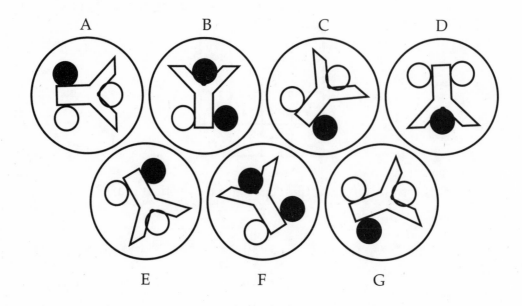

Place two three-letter segments together to form a shade

**ISE   SCA   YEL   LEW   CER   LET**

What number should replace the question mark?

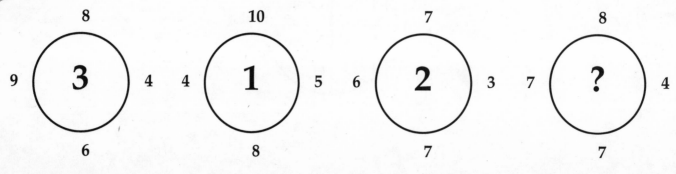

If the missing letters in the two circles below are correctly inserted they will form synonymous words. The words do not have to be read in a clockwise direction, but the letters are consecutive. What are the words and missing letters?

What word is an antonym of LAMBENT?

**A. FLICKERING**
**B. TWINKLING**
**C. STEADY**
**D. SLUGGISH**
**E. HEAVINESS**

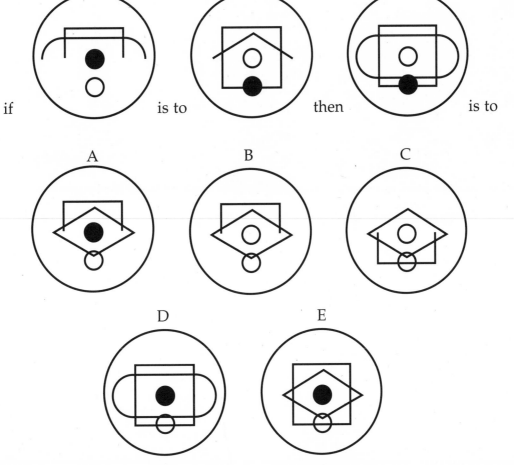

if ... is to ... then ... is to

A    B    C

D    E

# Answers

**1** E.
Opposite segments are mirror images except that black and white shading is reversed.

**2** Algeria. The words are: teA, niL, foG, tiE, baR, obI, and erA.

**3** D (179486).
The numbers were reordered as follows: sixth, third, first, seventh, fourth, fifth, second. Therefore the new order is:

| A | B | C | D | E | F | G |
|---|---|---|---|---|---|---|
| 9 | 6 | 7 | 4 | 8 | 1 | 2 |
| F | C | A | G | D | E | B |
| 1 | 7 | 9 | 2 | 4 | 8 | 6 |

**4** D.

**5** C (lectern, a stand).
The others are all types of book.

**6** 9.
(Top+Right) - (Bottom+Left) = Middle.

(73+3) - (39+28) = 76 - 67 = 9

Others are:

(72+55) - (83+37) = 127 - 120 = 7
and
(19+13) - (25+4) = 32 - 29 = 3

**7** Suggestive.

**8** Separated and decorator.

**9** B.

**10** 10. Please. Three letters of the left and right words transfer to the middle as follows:

| V | A | L | I | S | E |
|---|---|---|---|---|---|
|   | 4 |   |   | 5 | 3 |

| (P | L | E | A | S | E) |
|----|---|---|---|---|----|
| 1  | 2 | 3 | 4 | 5 | 6  |

| O | P | E | N | L | Y |
|---|---|---|---|---|---|
| 1 | 6 |   |   | 2 |   |

**11** Delight, offend.

**12** Phil is 48 years old. Ken is 72 and David is 32.

**13** E (routine : abnormal).
They are antonyms as are doubt and conviction.

**14** D.
The others all have identical pairs: A and H, B and G, C and F, and E and I.

# Answers

**15** MANS GUT (mustang).
The others are pumpkin (milk pup), blueberry (bury rebel), satsuma (USA mast) and mandarin (damn rain).

**16** 39.
The sums are (top + left) x right = middle. (7 + 6) [13] x 3 = 39.
Others are:
(7 + 5) [12] x 3 = 36;
(9 + 4) [13] x 2 = 26;
(8 + 5) [13] x 4 = 52.

**17** Gigolo.

**18** Ten.

**19** Daredevil.

**20** 3A.

**21** A (seizure).

**22** C (18).
Reading from the left along each row, (first column x second column) – third column = fourth column.
(7 x 4) [28] – 10 = 18.
Others are:
(6 x 2) [12] – 5 = 7;
(8 x 3) [24] – 17 = 7;
(9 x 2) [18] – 9 = 9.

**23** Sluggard. The missing letters are S and G.

**24** Ferret.

**25** D.
The others all have identical pairs: A and E, B and F, and C and G.

**26** Cerise.

**27** 2.
The sums are (top x left) ÷ (right x bottom) = middle.
(8 x 7) [56] ÷ (7 x 4) [28] = 2.
The others are
(8 x 9) [72] ÷ (4 x 6) [24] = 3;
(10 x 4) [40] ÷ (5 x 8) [40] = 1;
(7 x 6) [42] x (3 x 7) [21] = 2.

**28** Adherent, believer. The missing letters are H and N (adherent) and B and E (believer).

**29** C (steady).

**30** A. The black and white dots change position; the full square becomes a half-square and vice versa; and the oval becomes a diamond and vice versa (remaining a half-shape where appropriate).

Which of the following is the odd one out?

**1**

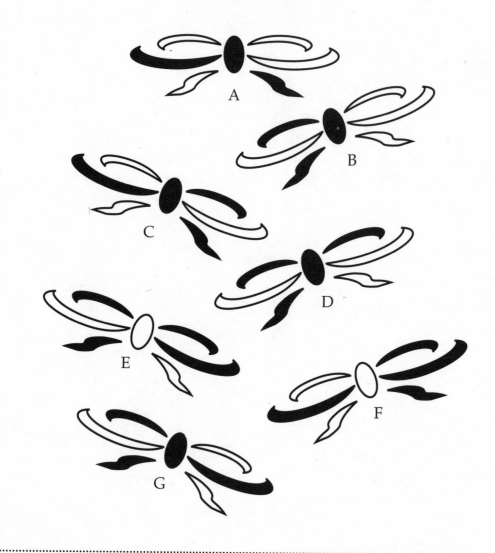

**2** GLOSSY METALS is an anagram of which well-known three-word phrase (3, 7, 2) which could also be "ready for the off."

What number should replace the question mark?

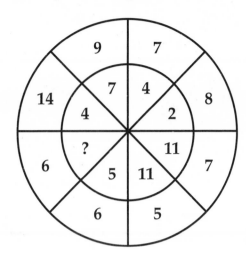

Start at a corner square and move in a clockwise spiral to the middle to spell out a nine-letter word. What are the missing letters?

| A | T | E |
|---|---|---|
|   |   | M |
| A | N | E |

What words are antonymous?

A. ABSTRUSE
B. DEFICIENT
C. PROFLIGATE
D. SECURE
E. CHASTE
F. EXOTIC

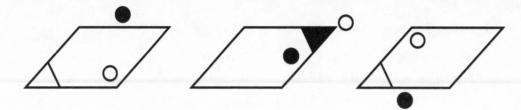

Which of the following, below, will continue the series above?

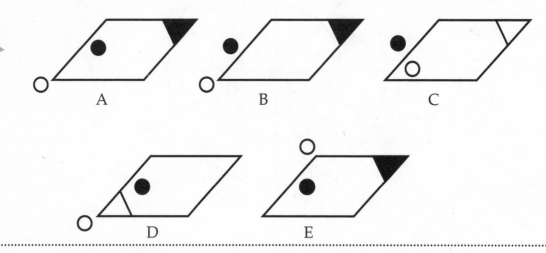

**6**

**7** A man returned from his greenhouse with a small basket of cherries. To his first friend he gave half his cherries, plus half a pair of cherries, to his second he gave half of what he had left, plus half a pair of cherries, and to the third he gave half of what he had left, plus half a pair of cherries. This meant he had no cherries left. How many did he start with?

**8** What word will go with the following series?

**GAMMON     ACHE     TRACK     ?**

A. MEAT
B. WARD
C. FIND
D. SMOOTH
E. KIND

**9** TURRET is to WATCHTOWER as DONJON is to:

A. RAMPART
B. PORTCULLIS
C. COURTYARD
D. KEEP
E. DITCH

## 10

What number will replace the question mark?

1  2  3  7  22  ?

A. 52
B. 68
C. 126
D. 154
E. 155

## 11

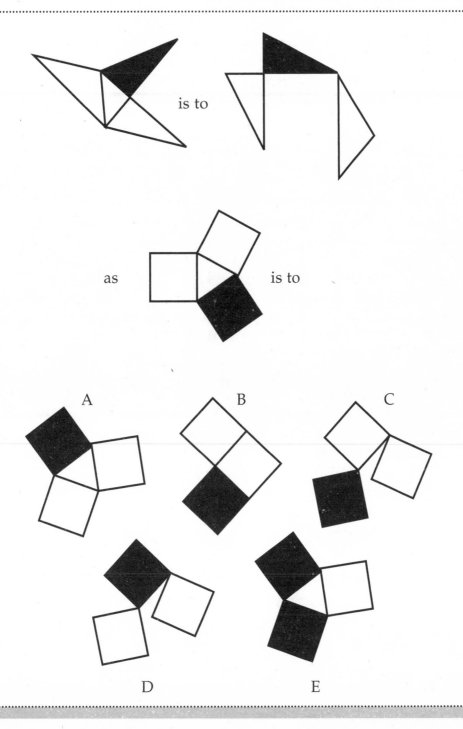

is to

as

is to

A          B          C

D          E

**12**

Which of the following is the odd one out?

> A. CASKET
> B. CARBOY
> C. DECANTER
> D. DEMIJOHN
> E. AMPULLA

**13**

What word is a synonym of LOGISTICS?

> A. VALIDITY
> B. MANAGEMENT
> C. STRENGTH
> D. RESOURCES
> E. RECORD

**14**

What number should replace the question mark?

```
1 7 5 9 5 7
6 4 8 1 4 4
2 3 2 ? 9 2
9 1 2 3 3 5
2 6 5 4 3 7
```

**15**

If the missing letters in the two circles below are correctly inserted they will form antonymous words. The words do not have to be read in a clockwise direction, but the letters are consecutive. What are the words and missing letters?

**16**

What number should replace the question mark?

**91  73⅝  56¼  38⅞  ?**

**17**

A word can be placed in the brackets that has the same meaning as the words outside. What is it?

**VIOLIN  ( • • • • • • )  SWINDLE**

**18**

Which of the following is always an ingredient of CURACAO?

**A. PLUMS
B. LEMON PEEL
C. ORANGE PEEL
D. CHERRIES
E. LIME**

**19**

Find a six-letter word made up of only the following four letters?

**P O
E H**

Which of the following will replace the question mark and complete the series?

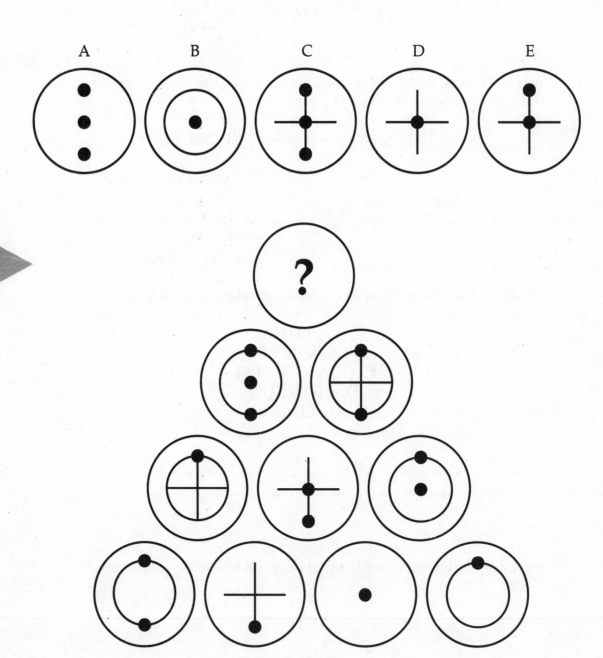

If the missing letters in the two circles below are correctly inserted they will form synonymous words. The words do not have to be read in a clockwise direction, but the letters are consecutive. What are the words and missing letters?

**21**

What number should replace the question mark?

**22**

| 7 | 5 | 9 | 18 |
| 6 | 3 | 7 | 21 |
| 4 | 3 | 9 | ? |
| 7 | 4 | 8 | 24 |

What word can be placed in front of the other five to form five new words? Each dot represents a letter.

**23**

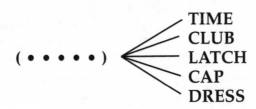

( • • • • • ) TIME
CLUB
LATCH
CAP
DRESS

**24**

If the missing letters in the circle below are correctly inserted they will form an eight-letter word. The word will not have to be read in a clockwise direction, but the letters are consecutive. What is the word and missing letters?

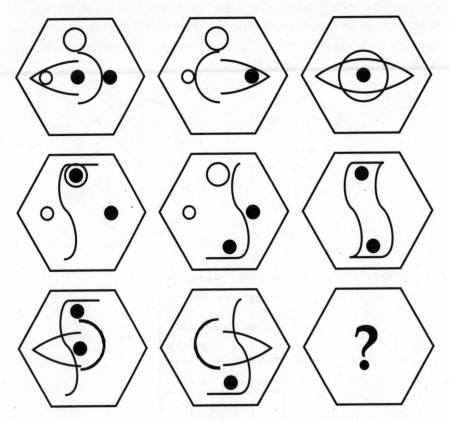

Which of the hexagons below should replace the question mark above?

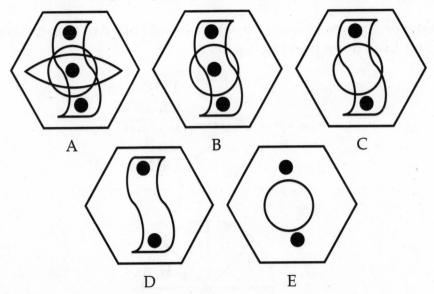

A    B    C

D    E

What number should replace the question mark?

2   −5⅞   −13¾   ?   −29½   −37⅜

**27** What two words are antonymous?

> A. GRAND
> B. BALEFUL
> C. ECONOMICAL
> D. CLEAN
> E. SHARP
> F. SULLY

**28** What word is closest in meaning to feisty?

> A. HOLY
> B. MALEVOLENT
> C. MEAN
> D. GENEROUS
> E. EXCITABLE

**29** Place two three-letter segments together to form a tree.

**CHE   DEN   OAK   LOW   LIN   POP**

 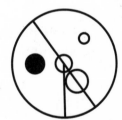  

Which of the circles below will continue the sequence above?

**30**

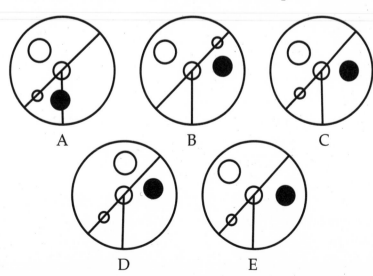

69

# Answers

**1** D.
The others all have identical pairs: A and E, B and F, and C and G, except that black and white shading is reversed.

**2** All systems go.

**3** 4. The sum of diagonally opposite segments are the same. 6 + 4 = 8 + 2.

**4** Abatement.

**5** Profligate, chaste.

**6** A.
At each stage, the black circle rotates 90° clockwise and goes in and out of the parallelogram; the white circle rotates 90° anti- (counter) clockwise and also goes in and out of the parallelogram; the triangle rotates 180° and changes from black to white and vice versa.

**7** 7 pairs of cherries. He gave the 14 cherries to his friends as follows: To the first friend (half of 7) 3½ pairs + ½ a pair = 4 pairs (leaving 3 pairs).
To the second friend (half of 3) 1½ pairs + ½ a pair = 2 pairs (leaving 1 pair).
To the third friend (half of 1) ½ a pair + ½ a pair = 1 pair.

**8** Ward.
Each word can be prefixed by BACK, making backgammon, backache, backtrack, and backward.

**9** Keep.

**10** 155.
Consecutive numbers are multiplied together and 1 is added to the answer. 1 x 1 [1] + 1 = 2; 1 x 2 [2] + 1 = 3; 2 x 3 [6] + 1 = 7; 3 x 7 [21] + 1 = 22; 7 x 22 [154] + 1 = 155.

**11** C.
The left part transfers across to lie touching the original, uppermost right side.

**12** Casket. It is a box, the others are jars, normally made of glass.

**13** Management.

**14** 6.
The sum of the columns are, reading left to right: 20, 21, 22, 23, 24, 25.

**15** Intrepid, cautious.
The missing letters are: R and P (intrepid) and U twice (cautious).

# Answers

**16** ▸ 21½.
The number decreases by 17⅜
each time.

**17** ▸ Fiddle.

**18** ▸ C (orange peel).

**19** ▸ Hoopoe (a bird).

**20** ▸ D.
Different symbols in adjoining circles
on the same row are carried into the
circle between them in the row above.
Similar symbols in the same place are
dropped.

**21** ▸ Waxworks, effigies.
The missing letters are X and R
(waxworks) and F and G (effigies).

**22** ▸ 9.
Reading from left to right (first column
– second column) x third column =
fourth column. (4 – 3) [1] x 9 = 9. The
others are: (7 – 5) [2] x 9 = 18; (6 – 3) [3]
x 7 = 21; (7 – 4) [3] x 8 = 24.

**23** ▸ Night.

**24** ▸ Hipflask.
The missing letters are F and K.

**25** ▸ A.
Reading across rows and down
columns, unique elements in the first
two are transferred to the third (bottom
or right). Common elements disappear.

**26** ▸ –21⅝.
The number decreases by 7⅞
each time.

**27** ▸ F (sully) and D (clean).

**28** ▸ E (Excitable).

**29** ▸ Linden.

**30** ▸ C. At each stage, the long line rotates
45° clockwise, the short line rotates 180°
and all the circles rotate 90° clockwise.

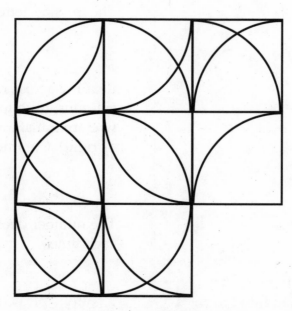

**1** ▶ Which of the following tiles will complete the square above?

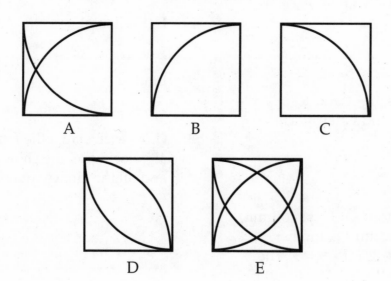

A                B                C

D                E

What number should replace the question mark?

| 12 | 33 | 21 | 12 |
|----|----|----|----|
| 27 | ?  | 31 | 27 |
| 15 | 25 | 10 | 15 |
| 12 | 33 | 21 | 12 |

A four-letter word can be added at the end of the following to make five new words. What is it?

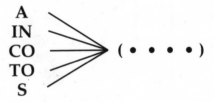

A
IN
CO
TO
S

( • • • • )

DREY is to SQUIRREL as HOLT is to:

A. OTTER
B. BADGER
C. BOAR
D. FERRET
E. MOLE

What is the value of $^{7}/_{9} \div ^{1}/_{3}$?

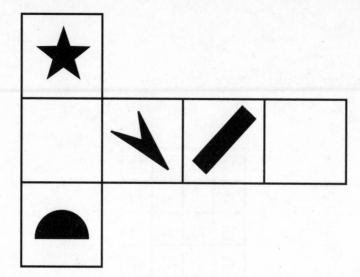

When the above is folded into a cube, only one of the following can be produced. Which one is it?

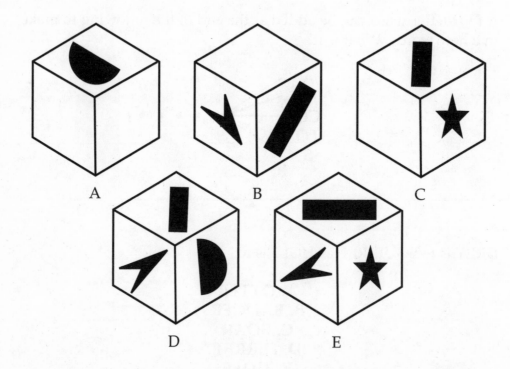

A       B       C

D       E

Start at a corner square and move in a clockwise spiral to the middle to spell out a nine-letter word. What are the missing letters?

| O |   | E |
|---|---|---|
| E | C | T |
|   | I | R |

**8**

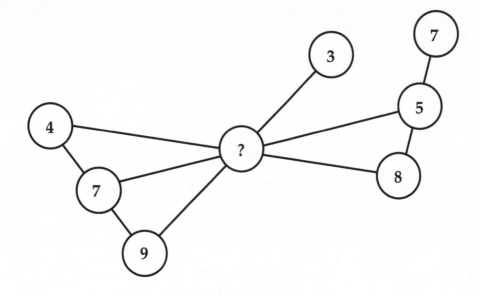

What number should replace the question mark?

**9**

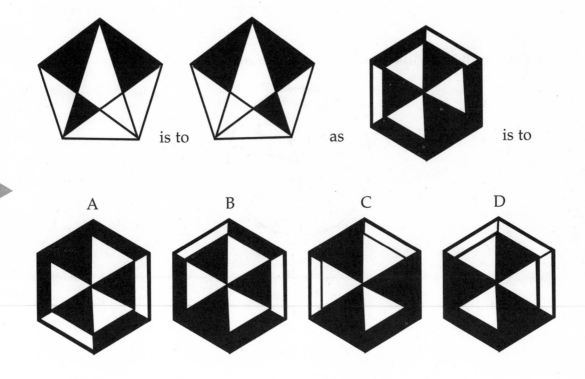

**10**

Two American soldiers meet on a bridge. One is the father of the other one's son. What is their relationship?

**11**

What two words are antonymous?

**A. ONEROUS**
**B. EFFICACIOUS**
**C. FIRM**
**D. SAD**
**E. UNAVAILING**
**F. CORRUPT**

**12**

What word is the odd one out?

**A. MILKSOP**
**B. COWARD**
**C. TRAITOR**
**D. WEAKLING**
**E. NAMBY-PAMBY**

**13**

What number will replace the question mark?

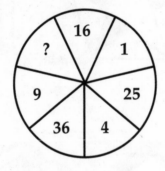

**A. 46**
**B. 45**
**C. 47**
**D. 49**
**E. 0**

**14**

What two words are closest in meaning?

**A. HASTY**
**B. INDIRECTLY**
**C. CARELESSLY**
**D. OBLIQUELY**
**E. CAREFULLY**
**F. SLICK**

**15**

What word is the odd one out?

A. REGENERATE
B. REGURGITATE
C. REVITALIZE
D. RESUSCITATE
E. REANIMATE

**16**

What number should replace the question mark?

5   1   2½   2½   0   4   −2½   ?

**17**

A word can be placed in the brackets that has the same meaning as the words outside. Each dot represents a letter. What is it?

MANAGER   ( • • • • )   STUD

**18**

What number should replace the question mark?

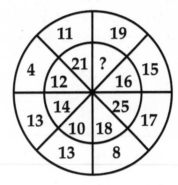

**19**

Which of the following is not a type of wind?

A. MISTRAL
B. PAVANE
C. ZEPHYR
D. SIROCCO
E. MONSOON

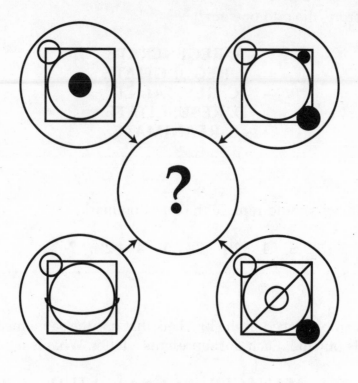

## 20

Each line and symbol that appears in the four outer circles, above, is transferred to the middle circle according how many times it appears, as follows:

**One time — it is transferred**
**Two times — it is possibly transferred**
**Three times — it is transferred**
**Four times — it is not transferred**

Which of the circles below should appear in the middle circle?

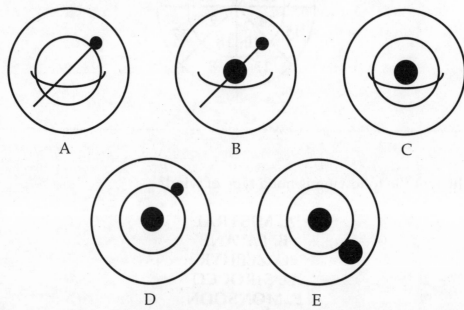

A          B          C

D          E

## 21

Place two three-letter segments together to form a coin.

**KOP   UDO   PIA   RUP   ESC   LIR**

## 22

What number should replace the question mark?

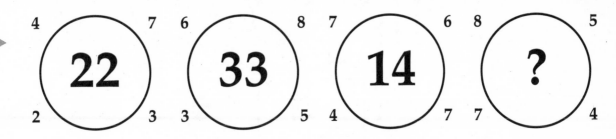

4  7
**22**
2  3

6  8
**33**
3  5

7  6
**14**
4  7

8  5
**?**
7  4

## 23

What word can be placed in front of the other five to form five new words or phrases, and some words may be hyphenated? Each dot represents a letter.

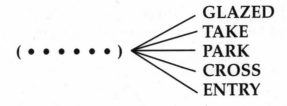

( • • • • • )
- GLAZED
- TAKE
- PARK
- CROSS
- ENTRY

## 24

If the missing letters in the circle below are correctly inserted they will form an eight-letter word. The word will not have to be read in a clockwise direction, but the letters are consecutive. What is the word and missing letters?

79

**25**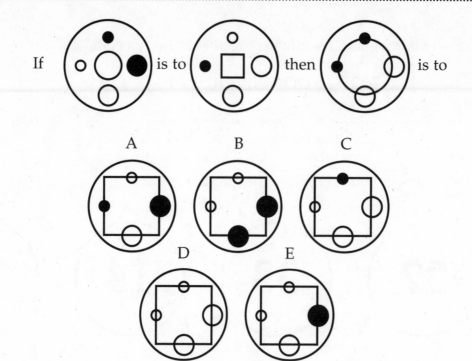

A     B     C

D     E

**26** If the missing letters in the two circles below are correctly inserted they will form synonymous words. The words do not have to be read in a clockwise direction, but the letters are consecutive. What are the words and missing letters?

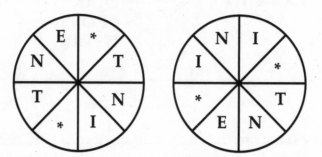

**27** Which of the following words is not a group noun (the name of a group of objects)?

> **A. COVEY**
> **B. SIEGE**
> **C. SHIELD**
> **D. SKULK**
> **E. CLOWDER**

**28**

What word is an antonym of NOCUOUS?

A. SYSTEMATIC
B. PAROCHIAL
C. HARMLESS
D. MERCURIAL
E. TRAUMATIC

**29**

Simplify the following and find x?

$$\frac{64 - 32}{1/8 - 1/16} = x$$

**30**

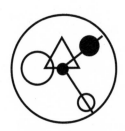

Which of the circles below will continue the sequence above?

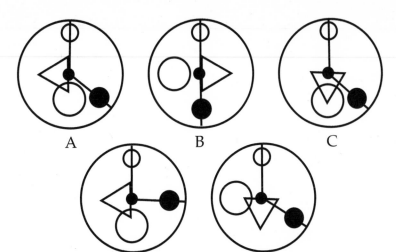

A          B          C

D          E

# Answers

**1** C.
Reading across columns and down rows, unique elements in the first two are transferred to the third (bottom or right). Common elements disappear.

**2** 58.
Looking across each row and down each column, the third and fourth numbers are the differences of the numbers in the two previous squares.

**3** Ward. The words made are: award, inward, coward, toward, and sward.

**4** Otter. A holt is an otter's home as a drey is a squirrel's home.

**5** 2⅓.
The sum can be rephrased as ⅞ x ¾ (or 3); 3 x ⅞ = 2¹⅛ (or 2⅓).

**6** A.

**7** Geometric.
The missing letters are G and M.

**8** 8.
The sum of each row of three digits is 20.

**9** B. The two figures are mirror images of each other.

**10** They are the son's mother and father.

**11** B (efficacious) and E (unavailing).

**12** C (traitor).

**13** D (49).
Alternate sectors increase by 1, 3, 5, 7, 9, 11, and 13.
They are also squares of 1, 2, 3, 4, 5, 6, and 7.

**14** B (indirectly) and D (obliquely).

**15** B (regurgitate, to vomit).
The others are to restore or revive

**16** 5½.
There are two series that alternate: one is – 2½, the other is + 1½.
Looking at the two series separately, – 2½ runs 5, 2½, 0, –2½;
+ 1½ goes 1, 2½, 4, 5½.

**17** Boss.

# Answers

**18** 16.
The sum of inner and diagonally opposite outer segments totals 29.

**19** Pavane (a dance).

**20** B.

**21** Escudo.

**22** 12.
In each case (top left x top right) – (bottom left x bottom right) = middle.
(8 x 5) [40] – (7 x 4) [28] = 12.
The others are:
(7 x 4) [28] – (2 x 3) [6] = 22;
(6 x 8) [48] – (3 x 5) [15] = 33;
(7 x 6) [42] – (4 x 7) [28] = 14.

**23** Double.

**24** Hijacker.
The missing letters are J and K.

**25** E.
The circle becomes a square; a black circle on the top becomes white; and black and white swap left to right.

**26** Ointment and liniment.
The missing letters are: O and M (ointment) and L and M (liniment).

**27** Shield.

**28** C (harmless).

**29** 512. 64 – 32 [32] ÷ ⅛ (²⁄₁₆) – ¹⁄₁₆ [¹⁄₁₆] can be rephrased as 32 x ¹⁶⁄₁ (16) = 512.

**30** C.
At each stage, the triangle rotates 180°, the large circle rotates 90° clockwise, the small white circle rotates 45° anti- (counter) clockwise, and the black circle rotates 90° anti- (counter) clockwise.

Four of the five pieces below can be fitted together to form a perfect square. What piece is the odd one out?

1

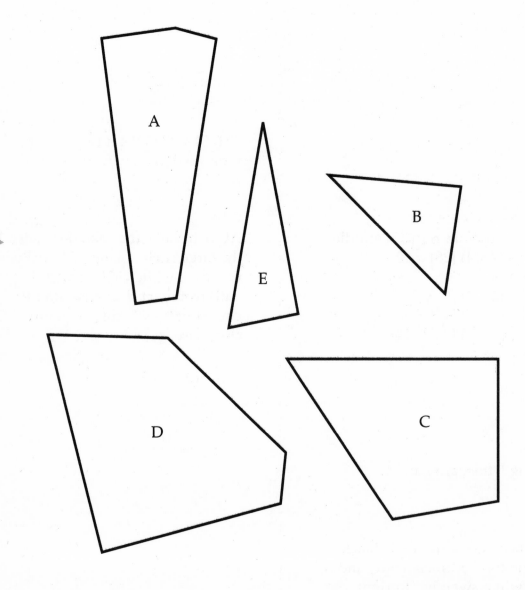

**ANGER  TENDER  DIRECT  RENTED  RANGE**

What word is missing from above?

> **A. GREEN**
> **B. FINAL**
> **C. CREDIT**
> **D. TRAIN**
> **E. DETECT**

What number should replace the question mark?

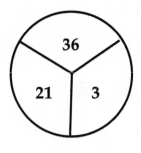 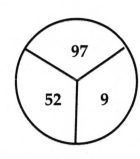 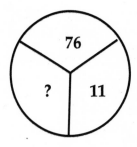

What word is a synonym of rectitude?

> **A. CORRUPTION**
> **B. REDRESS**
> **C. RESTORATION**
> **D. HONESTY**
> **E. REINSTATEMENT**

Bill's house is 10th from one end of the block and sixth from the other end. How many houses are there in the block?

Which shield, below, will replace the question mark above?

A       B       C       D       E

A three-word phrase, below, has had each word's initial letter removed. What is the phrase?

**OATCHN**

**NUMBER (RETURN) LETTER**

Following the same rules as above, what word should go in the brackets?

**TENDON ( • • • • • • ) LILIES**

Out of 100 people surveyed, 86 had an egg for breakfast, 75 had bacon, 62 had toast, and 82 had coffee. How many people, as least, must have had all four items?

What letter is immediately to the left of the letter three to the right of the letter immediately to the left of the letter three to the right of the letter B?

**A B C D E F G H**

Which of the following is the odd one out?

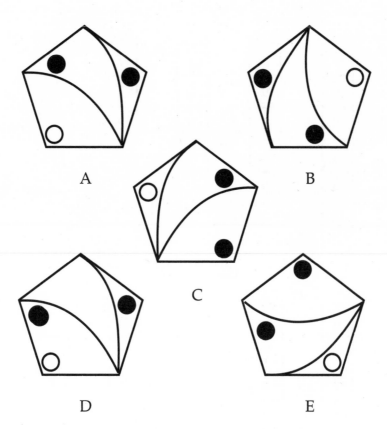

A

B

C

D

E

**12**

What two words are antonymous?

**A. CLUMSY**
**B. SLOW**
**C. CLOSE**
**D. EXOTIC**
**E. EXPERT**
**F. APPREHENSIVE**

**13**

What is the odd one out?

**A. MAJOR**
**B. ADMIRAL**
**C. COLONEL**
**D. BRIGADIER**
**E. GENERAL**

**14**

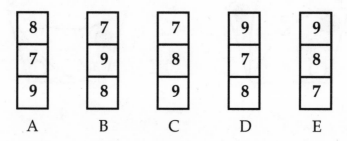

| 7 | 3 | 7 | ? |
| 6 | 9 | 6 | ? |
| 8 | 8 | 8 | ? |
| 2 | 6 | 9 |   |
| 9 | 7 |   |   |
| 3 |   |   |   |

Which of the boxes below will follow the sequence above?

| A | B | C | D | E |
|---|---|---|---|---|
| 8 | 7 | 7 | 9 | 9 |
| 7 | 9 | 8 | 7 | 8 |
| 9 | 8 | 9 | 8 | 7 |

**15**

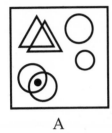  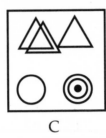  

A    B    C    D    E

Into which of the boxes A, B, C, D, or E, can a dot be placed so that both dots will meet the same conditions as in the top box?

**16**

A word can be placed in the brackets that has the same meaning as the words outside. What is it?

**PENALTY ( • • • • )  EXCELLENT**

**17**

What number should replace the question mark?

**7  –5  2  1  –3  7  –8  13  ?  19**

**18**

Place two three-letter segments together to form a profession.

**BUR  SOL  GAR  DEN  SAR  VAN**

What word can be placed in front of the other five to form five new words or phrases? Each dot represents a letter.

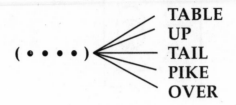

TABLE
UP
TAIL
PIKE
OVER

Each of the nine squares in the grid marked 1A to 3C should incorporate all of the items which are shown in the squares of the same letter and number, at the left and top, respectively. For example, 2B should incorporate all of the symbols that are in squares 2 and B. One square, however, is incorrect. Which one is it?

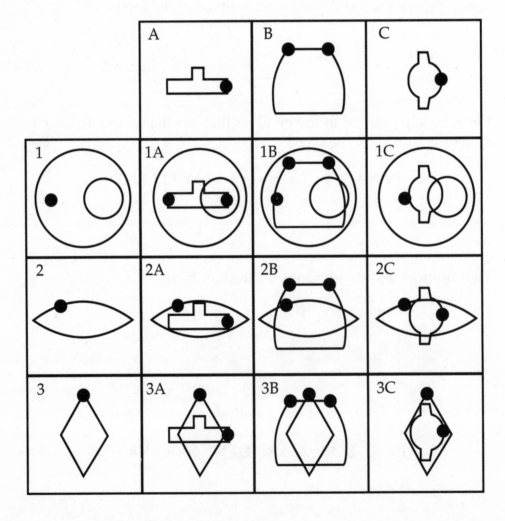

**21**

Find a six-letter word made up of only the following four letters?

T E
P O

**22**

What number should replace the question mark?

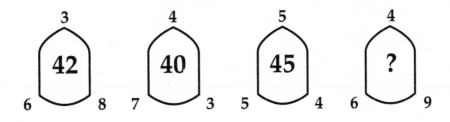

3
42
6   8

4
40
7   3

5
45
5   4

4
?
6   9

**23**

What is a LEMAN?

A. A PARAMOUR
B. AN ANIMAL
C. A NOOSE
D. A BODICE
E.. A SPINNAKER

**24**

If the missing letters in the circle below are correctly inserted they will form an eight-letter word. The word will not have to be read in a clockwise direction, but the letters are consecutive. What is the word and missing letters?

Which of the following is the odd one out?

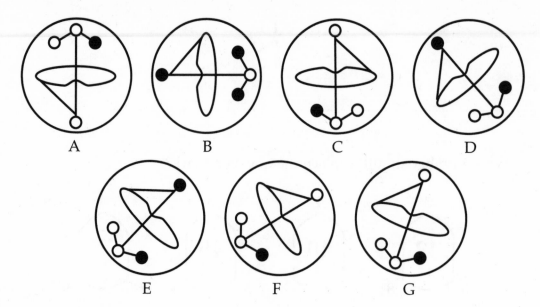

A    B    C    D

E    F    G

25

What word is a synonym of bathos?

**A. DIFFIDENT**
**B. DEPTH**
**C. DISTORTION**
**D. DEFLATE**
**E. DEFECTION**

26

If the missing letters in the two circles below are correctly inserted they will form synonymous words. The words do not have to be read in a clockwise direction, but the letters are consecutive. What are the words and missing letters?

27

MOOD TANS is an anagram of what eight-letter word?

28

## 29

What number should replace the question mark?

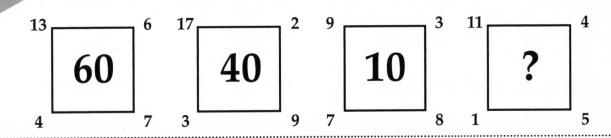

Which of the circles A, B, C, D, or E, should replace the question mark below?

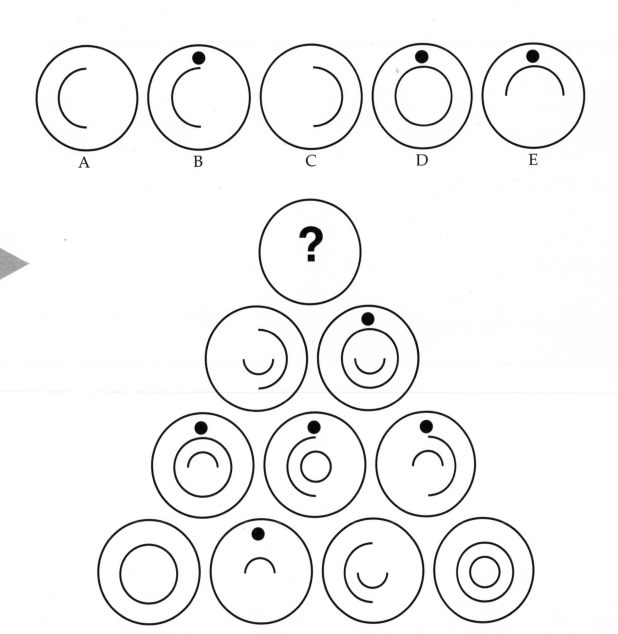

# Answers

**1** C.

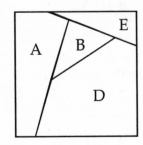

**2** C (credit).
Credit is an anagram of direct as is anger of range, and tender is of rented.

**3** 21. In each case (top – left) ÷ 5 = right.
(76 – 21) [55] ÷ 5 = 11.
The others are:
(36 – 21) [15] ÷ 5 = 3;
(97 – 52) [45] ÷ 5 = 9.

**4** Honesty.

**5** 15.

**6** B.
Reading across columns and down rows of shields, common elements with the same shading in the first two are transferred to the third (bottom or right) and change shading. Unique elements disappear.

**7**

**8** To catch on.
Silent. Three letters of the left and right words transfer to the middle as follows:

T  E  N  D  O  N
6  4           5

(S  I  L  E  N  T)
 1  2  3  4  5  6

L  I  L  I  E  S
   2  3        1

**9** 5. Add the differences between 100 and 86, 75, 62 and 82, then subtract this total from the original 100.
(14 + 25 + 38 + 18) = 95;
100 – 95 = 5.

**10** F.

**11** D. The others all have identical pairs: A and B, and C and E.

**12** A (clumsy) and E (expert).

**13** B (admiral, a naval rank).
The others are all army ranks.

**14** E. The order of the column is reversed and the lowest digit is removed each time.

# Answers

**15** D.
One dot will appear in a enclosed small circle and another in the link between two larger circles.

**16** Fine.

**17** −13. There are two alternate series, − 5 and + 6. The numbers are:
7, 2, −3, −8, −13; −5, 1, 7, 13, 19.

**18** Bursar.

**19** Turn.

**20** 1C.

**21** Poppet.

**22** 60.
The sums are:
(top x left) + (top x right) = middle.
(4 x 6) [24] + (4 x 9) [36] = 60.
Others are:
(3 x 6) [18] + (3 x 8) [24] = 42;
(4 x 7) [28] + (4 x 3) [12] = 40;
(5 x 5) [25] + (5 x 4) [20] = 45.

**23** A (a paramour).

**24** Gangrene.
The missing letter is G twice.

**25** B. The others all have identical pairs: A and C, D and E, and F and G.

**26** C (distortion).

**27** Impolite and insolent.
The missing letters are: M and L (impolite) and S and T (insolent).

**28** Mastodon.

**29** 30.
The sums are: (top left − bottom right) x (bottom left + top right) = middle.
(11 − 5) [6] x (1 + 4) [5] = 30.
Others are:
(13 − 7) [6] x (4 + 6) [10] = 60;
(17 − 9) [8] x (3 + 2) [5] = 40;
(9 − 8) [1] x (7 + 3) [10] = 10.

**30** B. Different symbols/lines in adjoining circles on the same row are carried into the circle between them in the row above. Similar symbols/lines in the same place are dropped.

## 1

What comes next in this sequence?

| A | B | C | D | E |

## 2

What two words are antonyms?

**A. BARE**
**B. TINY**
**C. SAFE**
**D. PRODIGIOUS**
**E. ABUSIVE**
**F. FRUGAL**

**3**

What number is the odd one out?

A. 382618
B. 589411
C. 213787
D. 528572
E. 654346

**4**

Find the starting point and move from square to adjoining square, horizontally or vertically, but not diagonally, to spell a 12-letter word, using each letter once only. What are the missing letters?

| A |   | P |
|---|---|---|
| R | T | O |
| N | I | L |
| I | S |   |

**5**

Simile is to comparison as onomatopoeia is to:

A. REPETITION
B. SOUND
C. VERSION
D. UNDERSTATEMENT
E. EXAGGERATION

6. Which of the following is the odd one out?

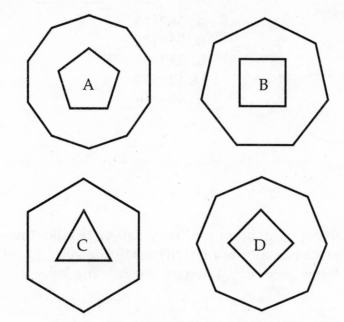

| A |   | E |   | J |
|---|---|---|---|---|
| D |   | ? |   | M |
| H |   | L |   | Q |

What letter should replace the question mark?

What number comes next in this sequence?

**1   3   8   19   42   ?**

HALTED CAR is an anagram of what nine-letter word?

**10**

| | 72 | |
|---|---|---|
| 46 | 16 | 51 |
| | 34 | |

| | 96 | |
|---|---|---|
| 38 | 18 | 43 |
| | 12 | |

| | 28 | |
|---|---|---|
| 14 | ? | 16 |
| | 11 | |

What number should replace the question mark?

**11**

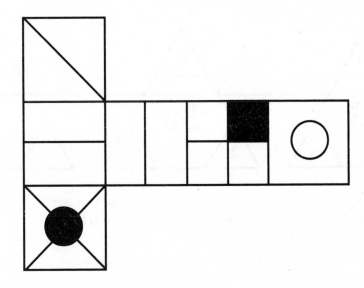

When the above is folded to form a cube, just one of the following below can be produced. What one is it?

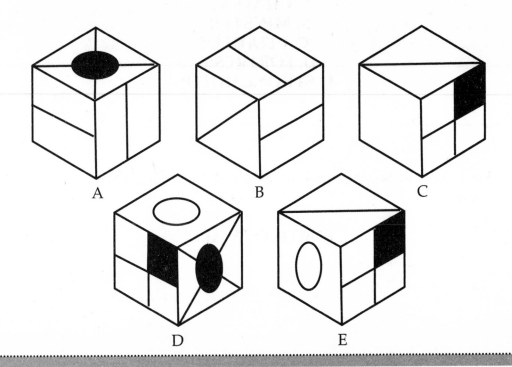

A    B    C

D    E

**12**

What two words are synonymous?

A. PENALTY
B. HINT
C. REQUEST
D. ORDER
E. MOTIVE
F. MAXIMUM

**13**

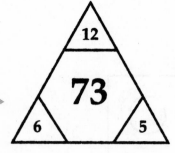 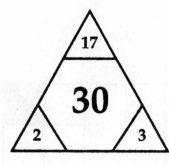 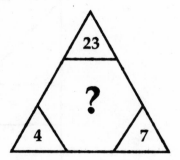

What number should replace the question mark?

**14**

What is the odd one out?

A. CHATEAU
B. MINSTER
C. CITADEL
D. FORTRESS
E. STRONGHOLD

**15**

Find two words with different spellings, but sound alike, that can mean:

**PORTICO / WALK**

**16**

What number should replace the question mark?

22  14¼  6½  ?  −9

**17**

Insert a word in the brackets that completes the first word and starts the second one. Each dot represents a letter.

TRAM  ( • • • • )  AGE

**18**

Place two three-letter segments together to form a vehicle.

TER  WAY  SKY  DRO  VER  CAR

**19**

A word can be placed in the brackets that has the same meaning as the words outside. What is it?

AVERAGE  ( • • • • )  STINGY

Which of the hexagons at the bottom, A, B, C, D, or E, should replace the question mark below?

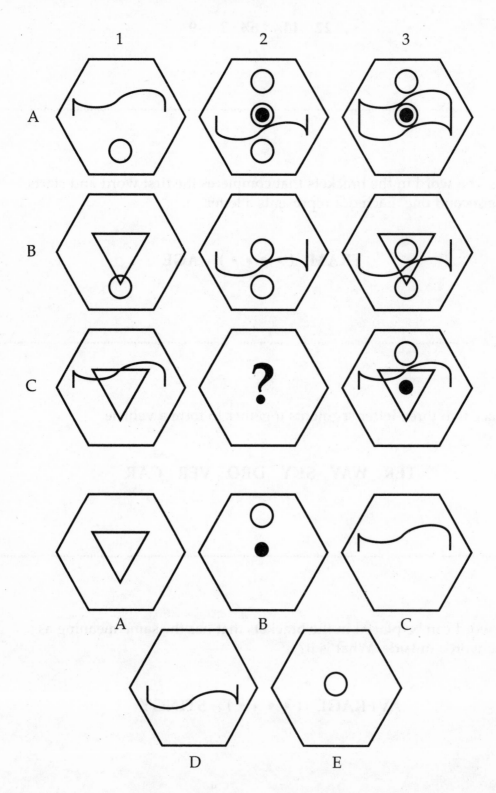

**21**

If the missing letters in the circle below are correctly inserted they will form an eight-letter word. The word will not have to be read in a clockwise direction, but the letters are consecutive. What is the word and missing letters?

**22**

Find a six-letter word made up of only the following four letters.

L E
O G

**23**

What word can be placed in front of the other five to form five new words? Each dot represents a letter.

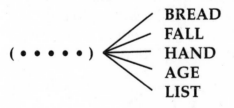

**24**

What number should replace the question mark?

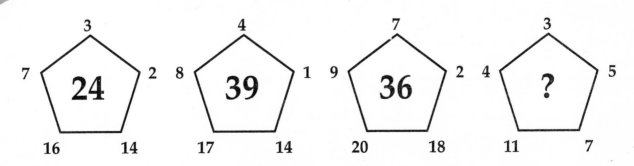

Which of the following is the odd one out?

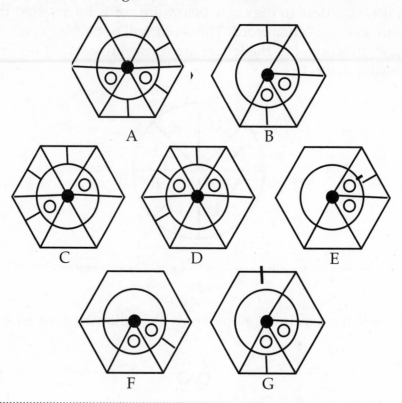

A      B

C      D      E

F      G

25

26

NEAR BUMP is an anagram of what eight-letter word?

If the missing letters in the two circles below are correctly inserted they will form synonymous words. The words do not have to be read in a clockwise direction, but the letters are consecutive. What are the words and missing letters?

27

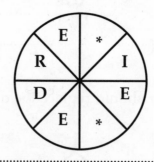

Which of the following is not an occupation?

**A. VESPIARY**
**B. BAILIFF**
**C. COURIER**
**D. VINTNER**
**E. BALLERINA**

28

**29** ▶

What is a GIMCRACK?

A. BLOW
B. BAUBLE
C. JAUNTY
D. CRACKER
E. PRESS

Which of the circles below should replace the question mark below?

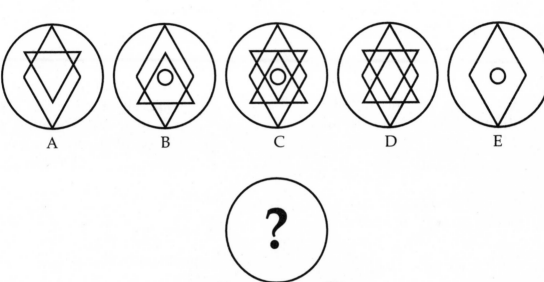

A     B     C     D     E

**30** ▶

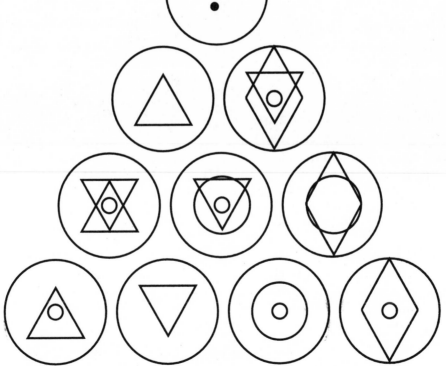

# Answers

**1** D.
All three shapes move down one place at each stage and the star goes from black to white and vice versa.

**2** B (tiny) and D (prodigious).

**3** D (528572).
The others, if split in half and added as two three-digits numbers, would total 1000. 528 + 572 = 1100.

**4** Trampolinist. The missing letters are, reading from top to bottom: M and T.

**5** Sound.

**6** B.
The number of sides of the inner figure should be half those of the outer ones. In the case of B, there is a square inside a seven-sided figure.

**7** H.
Reading down each column, the letter advances three, then four places in the alphabet. Reading across, the difference is four, then five places.

**8** 89.
Double the previous number, then add 1, 2, 3, 4, and 5, respectively.

**9** Cathedral.

**10** 12.
The sum of digits of the left and right numbers and also the top and bottom ones equals the middle number.
1 + 4 + 1 + 6 = 12; 2 + 8 + 1 + 1 = 12.

**11** C.

**12** C (request) and D (order).

**13** 88.
The sum is: $left^2 + right^2 + top = middle$.
$4^2$ [16] + $7^2$ [49] + 23 = 88.

Others are:
$6^2$ [36] + $5^2$ [25] + 12 = 73;
$2^2$ [4] + $3^2$ [9] + 17 = 30.

**14** B (minster). The rest are types of military buildings; a minster is a religious one.

**15** Gate and gait.

# Answers

**16** −1¼. Subtract 7¾ at each stage.

**17** Line.

**18** Drosky
(a Russian two- or four-wheeled cart).

**19** Mean.

**20** B.
Reading across columns and down rows, unique elements in the first two are transferred to the third (bottom or right). Common elements disappear.

**21** Tribunal.
The missing letters are T and B.

**22** Goggle.

**23** Short.

**24** 48.
The sums are (bottom left − bottom right) x (sum of top three numbers) = middle.
(11 − 7) [4] x (4 + 3 + 5) [12] = 48.
Others are:
(16 − 14) [2] x (7 + 3 + 2) [12] = 24;
(17 − 14) [3] x (8 + 4 + 1) [13] = 39;
(20 − 18) [2] x (4 + 3 + 5) [12] = 36.

**25** C.
The others all have identical pairs: A and D, B and G, and E and F.

**26** Penumbra.

**27** Imposter and deceiver.
The missing letters are P and T (imposter) and C and V (deceiver).

**28** A (vespiary, a wasp's nest).

**29** B (bauble).

**30** C.
Different symbols in adjoining circles on the same row are carried into the circle between them in the row above. Similar symbols in the same place are dropped.

# Test Seven

**1**

ROWS   (SOFTWARE)   FATE
?      (COMPLETE)    MELT

Which word below should replace the question mark above?

A. COME
B. POET
C. COPE
D. LOPE
E. CODE

**2**

ISLAND : WATER

Which pair of words below have the same relationship as the words above?

A. ORCHARD : TREES
B. MEADOW : GRASS
C. BOOK : COVER
D. OASIS : SAND
E. HEM : FRINGE

**3**

What word is an antonym of ARISTOCRATIC?

A. UNKIND
B. PATRICIAN
C. LIBERAL
D. POOR
E. PLEBIAN

**4** How many minutes is it before 10.00 pm if, 50 minutes ago, it was four times as many minutes past 7.00 pm?

**5**

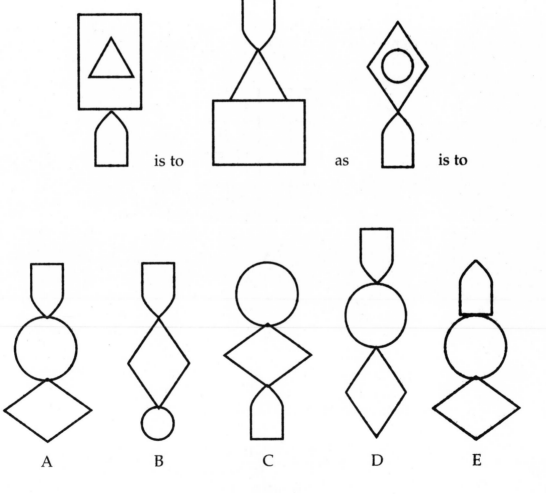

**6**

Which of the five boxes below is most like the box above?

 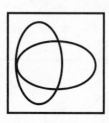 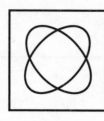  

A      B      C      D      E

**7**

What number should replace the question mark?

| 7 | 4 | 9 | 2 |
|---|---|---|---|
| 3 | 1 | 1 | 3 |
| 4 | 7 | 6 | 5 |
| 2 | 2 | ? | 4 |

A. 0
B. 1
C. 2
D. 3
E. 4

**8**

What would describe STERNUTATION?

A. Heavy breathing
B. The act of sneezing
C. Shouting loudly
D. A strict upbringing
E. Bringing up the rear

Which of the pentagons below will replace the question mark above?

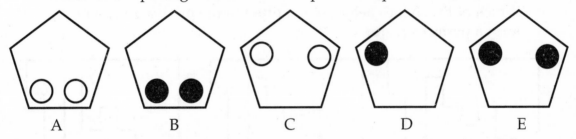

A     B     C     D     E

```
            A
        A   S   A
      A S   N   S A
    A S N   E   N S A
  A S N E   M   E N S A
    A S N   E   N S A
      A S   N   S A
        A   S   A
            A
```

In how many ways can the word MENSA be read? Start at the central letter M and move to an adjoining letter vertically or horizontally, but not diagonally.

$$7240 : 905$$
$$2456 : 307$$

Which pair of numbers below have the same relationship as the numbers above?

- A. 8056 : 98
- B. 3216 : 402
- C. 4824 : 36
- D. 9872 : 108
- E. 7218 : 94

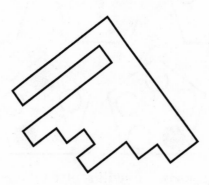

Which of the shapes below, when fitted to the piece above, will form a perfect square?

A   B   C

D   E

**13**

What word is the odd one out?

> A. VERIFY
> B. MONITOR
> C. AUTHENTICATE
> D. SUBSTANTIATE
> E. VALIDATE

**14**

Find two words with different spellings, but sound alike, that can mean:

**BOUNTY / MEDDLES**

**15**

What two words words are synonymous?

> A. FRACAS
> B. PALAVER
> C. SKIRMISH
> D. PAROXYSM
> E. COERCION
> F. FRACTURE

**16**

What number should replace the question mark?

$$2 \quad -\tfrac{1}{3} \quad \tfrac{1}{18} \quad ? \quad \tfrac{1}{648}$$

> A. $\tfrac{1}{108}$
> B. $\tfrac{1}{324}$
> C. $-\tfrac{1}{324}$
> D. $-\tfrac{1}{108}$
> E. $\tfrac{1}{36}$

**17**

Place two three-letter segments together to form an item of clothing.

**ORA   TER   GOT   ROS   FED   RUF**

## 18

If the missing letters in the circle below are correctly inserted they will form an eight-letter word. The word will not have to be read in a clockwise direction, but the letters are consecutive. What is the word and missing letters?

## 19

What word can be placed in front of the other five to form five new words? Each dot represents a letter.

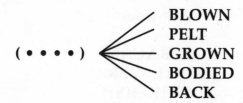

BLOWN
PELT
GROWN
BODIED
BACK

## 20

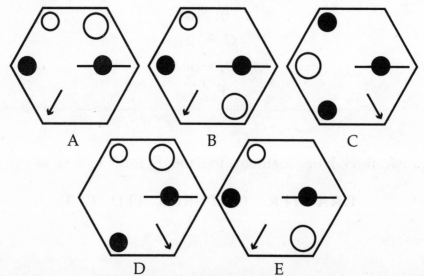

Which of the hexagons below should replace the question mark above?

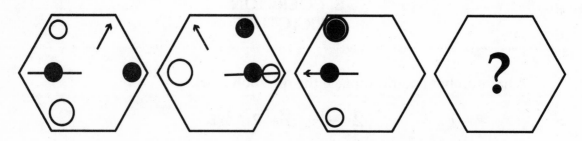

If the missing letters in the two circles below are correctly inserted they will form synonymous words. The words do not have to be read in a clockwise direction, but the letters are consecutive. What are the words and missing letters?

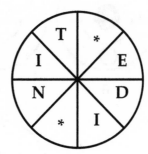

What word is a synonym of RAILLERY?

**A. CENSURE**
**B. SHELVES**
**C. FENCING**
**D. BANTER**
**E. VEHEMENCE**

A word can be placed in the brackets that has the same meaning as the words outside. What is it?

**COMPUTER INSTRUMENT ( • • • • • ) RODENT**

What is the odd one out?

**A. BEETLE**
**B. BEE**
**C. WASP**
**D. SPIDER**
**E. ANT**

Which of the circles, A, B, C, D, or E, should replace the question mark below?

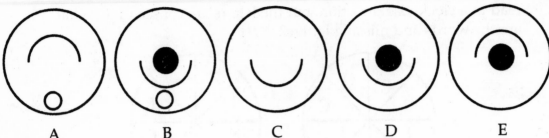

A       B       C       D       E

**25**

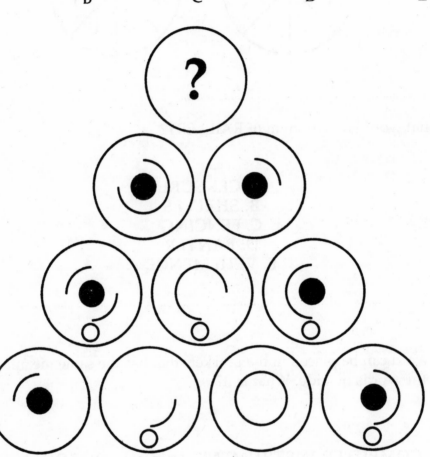

**26**  Find a six-letter word made up of only the following four letters?

O W
L I

**27**  What is the value of x?

$$(3 \times 14 \div 2) + 6 + 56 = x$$

**28**

What word is a synonym of LUCUBRATION?

A. STUDY
B. OIL
C. DELIGHT
D. DECEPTION
E. PERCEPTION

**29**

What word is not an antonym of HEINOUS?

A. ODIOUS
B. ATROCIOUS
C. PRAISEWORTHY
D. AWFUL
E. NEFARIOUS

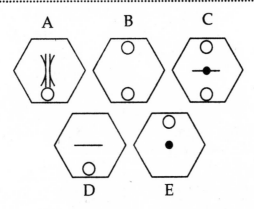

**30**

Which of the hexagons above should replace the question mark below?

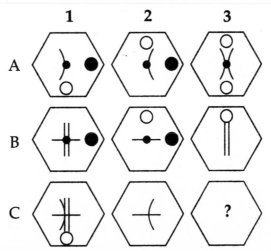

# Answers

**1** ▸ C (cope).
The two words outside the brackets form an anagram so removing "melt" from "complete" will leave the letters to make cope.

**2** ▸ D (oasis : sand).
Sand entirely surrounds an oasis as water surrounds an island.

**3** ▸ E (plebian).

**4** ▸ 26 minutes.

**5** ▸ A.
The top two items separate; the larger one rotates 90° clockwise and moves to the bottom, and the smaller one becomes large and goes in the middle. The bottom item rotates 180° and moves to the top.

**6** ▸ C.
It is the only one with vertical, horizontal, and diagonal symmetry.

**7** ▸ A (0).
The sum of the two left columns is the same as the sum of the two right columns. Also, the 1st and 3rd columns have the same values as do the 2nd and 4th columns. The same applies to the rows.

**8** ▸ B (the act of sneezing).

**9** ▸ C.
Identical symbols, including shading, in adjoining pentagons on the same row are carried into the pentagon between them in the row above. Different symbols in the same place are dropped.

**10** ▸ 60 ways.

**11** ▸ B (3216 : 42).
The left pair of digits and the right pair of digits are both divided by eight.

**12** ▸ B.

**13** ▸ B (monitor). The others mean to prove; monitor is to check.

**14** ▸ Prize and pries .

**15** ▸ A (fracas) and C (skirmish).

**16** ▸ D ($-\frac{1}{108}$).
Multiply by $-\frac{1}{6}$ at each stage.

# Answers

**17** Fedora (a wide-brimmed hat).

**18** Jerrycan.
The missing letters are J and R.

**19** Full.

**20** A.
At each stage the large white circle rotates 60° clockwise, the small white circle rotates 120° clockwise, the black dot with a line rotates 180°, and the arrow and the small black circle both rotate 60° anti- (counter) clockwise.

**21** Occasion and incident. The missing letters are C and N in both cases.

**22** D (banter).

**23** Mouse.

**24** D (spider, which has eight legs). The others are all bugs with six legs.

**25** C.
Different symbols in adjoining circles on the same row are carried into the circle between them in the row above. Similar symbols in the same place are dropped.

**26** Willow.

**27** 83.

**28** A (study).

**29** C (praiseworthy).

**30** A.
Reading across columns and down rows, unique elements in the first two are transferred to the third (bottom or right). Common elements disappear.

# Test Eight

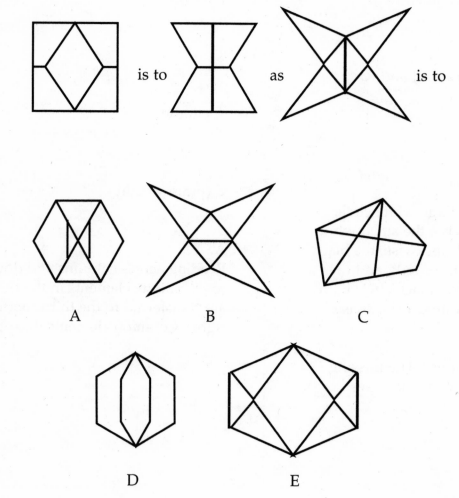

**1**

**2** If one letter in each of the four words below is changed, a phrase can be found. What is it?

**AN SHE ODE LAND**

Complete the three-letter words, which, reading down, will reveal a bird.

**3**

E L ( • )
A I ( • )
S E ( • )
G E ( • )
S K ( • )
D I ( • )
P E ( • )
D U ( • )

**4**

A farmer with 240 yards of fencing wishes to enclose a rectangular area of the greatest possible size. What will be the greatest area surrounded?

Four of the pieces below can be fitted together to form a square. What is the odd one out?

**5**

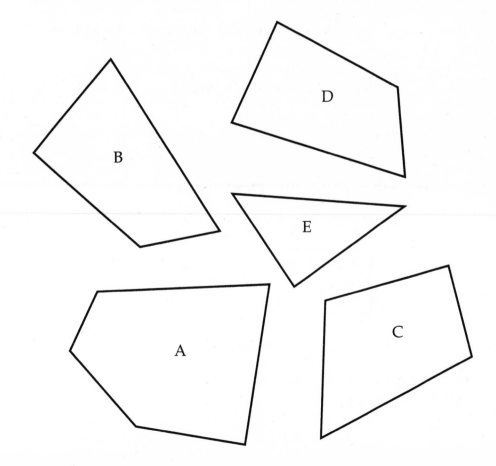

**6**

Start at a corner square and move in a clockwise spiral to the middle to spell out a nine-letter word.
What are the missing letters?

| F | | S |
|---|---|---|
| | E | C |
| A | N | I |

**7**

What word is a synonym of PRINCIPLE?

A. MAJESTY
B. AXIOM
C. COST
D. CAPITAL
E. LEADER

**8**

Find two words with different spellings, but sound alike, that can mean:

**RESIDUE / FORCE AWAY**

**9**

What number should replace the question mark?

| 5 | 6 | 1 |
|---|---|---|
| ? | 4 | 8 |
| 7 | 2 | 3 |

A. 0
B. 1
C. 2
D. 3
E. 4

**10**

A three-word phrase, below, has had each word's initial letter removed. What is the phrase?

**ETTASE**

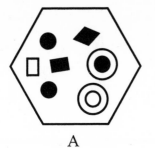 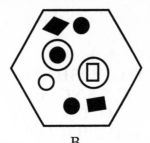 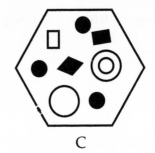

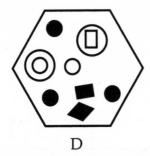 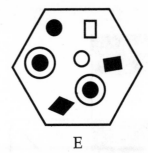

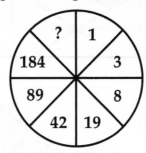

Which of the above hexagons is the odd one out?

What is the odd one out?

**A. PEW**
**B. PULPIT**
**C. FONT**
**D. BELFRY**
**E. AISLE**

What number should replace the question mark?

```
      ?  | 1
  184    |   3
   89    |   8
     42  | 19
```

What word is an antonym of CULPABLE?

**A. INNOCENT**
**B. LIABLE**
**C. ERUDITE**
**D. CREDULOUS**
**E. FLATTERING**

**15**

What word is a synonym of IMBROGLIO?

A. ENVY
B. FOOLISHNESS
C. TANGLE
D. SPECTACULAR
E. DUPLICITY

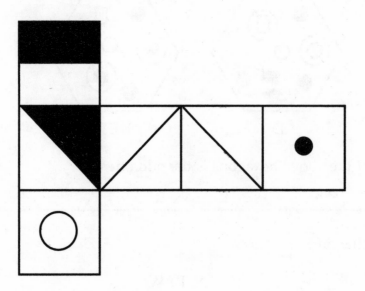

**16**

When the above is folded to form a cube, one of the figures below can be produced. What is it?

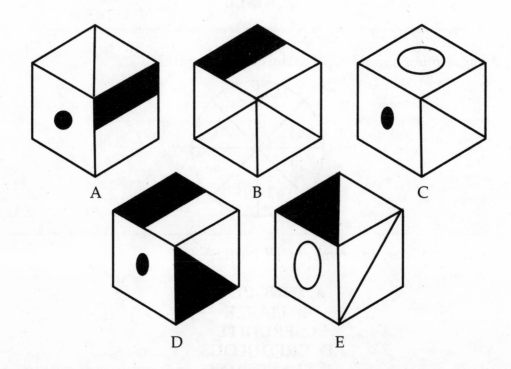

**17**

What word can be placed in front of the other five to form five new words or phrases? Each dot represents a letter.

( • • • • )  LIFE
HAUL
HORN
BOW
WINDED

**18**

Find a six-letter word made up of only the following four letters?

B E
U J

**19**

Which of the following is the odd one out?

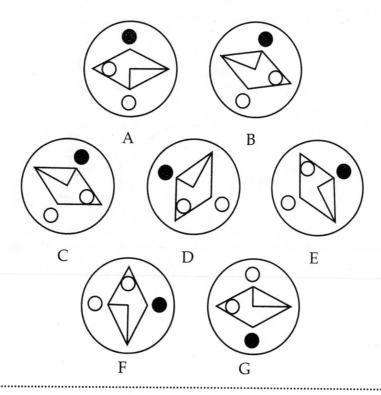

A    B

C    D    E

F    G

**20**

Place two three-letter segments together to form a weather term.

**HYR   MET   COM   ISO   ZEP   THE**

Which of the circles below should replace the question mark below?

21

A　　　B　　　C　　　D　　　E

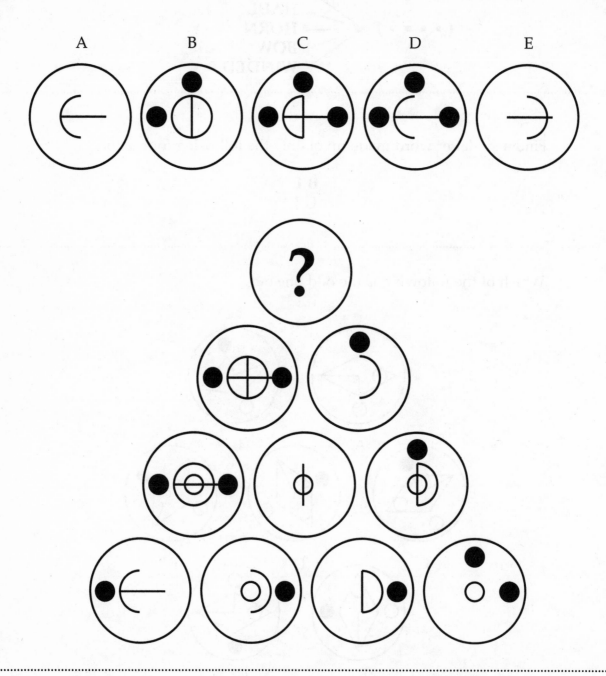

Which of the following is the opposite of TORPID?

22

A. SHALLOW
B. DROWSY
C. SLUGGISH
D. LETHARGIC
E. ENERGETIC

Which of the following words is the odd one out?

**A. CAPRICIOUS**
**B. FICKLE**
**C. UNSTABLE**
**D. SPURIOUS**
**E. INCONSTANT**

What number should complete the series and replace the question mark?

**73614   4637   764   ?**

A word can be placed in the brackets that has the same meaning as the words outside. What is it? Each dot represents a letter.

**A TRIFLE ( • • • • • • • • ) BALL GAME**

If the missing letters in the circle below are correctly inserted they will form an eight-letter word. The word will not have to be read in a clockwise direction, but the letters are consecutive. What is the word and missing letters?

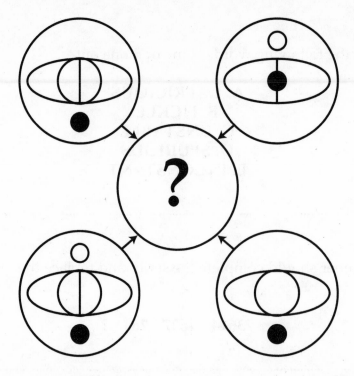

Each line and symbol that appears in the four outer circles, above, is transferred to the middle circle according to how many times it appears, as follows

**One time — it is transferred**
**Two times — it is possibly transferred**
**Three times — it is transferred**
**Four times — it is not transferred**

Which of the circles below should appear in the middle circle?

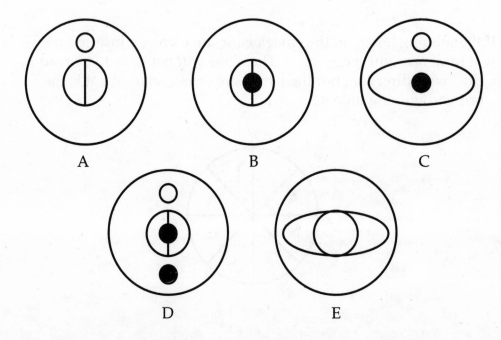

Find a 10-letter word using adjoining letters once each only.

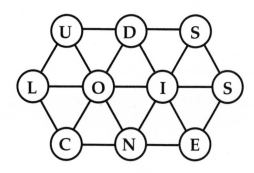

What word is a synonym of FARRAGO?

**A. A MIXTURE**
**B. A DANCE**
**C. A PLAIN**
**D. A TYPE OF WHEAT**
**E. A DINGO**

If the missing letters in the circle below are correctly inserted they will form an eight-letter word. The word will not have to be read in a clockwise direction, but the letters are consecutive. What is the word and missing letters?

# Answers

**1** E. The right and left halves of the figure switch positions as illustrated below:

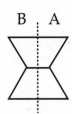

**2** On the one hand.

**3** Flamingo. The completed words are: elF, aiL, seA, geM, skI, diN, peG, duO.

**4** 3600 yards². Divide the 240 yards by 4 to get 60 yards each side, so 60 x 60 = 3600.

**5** D.

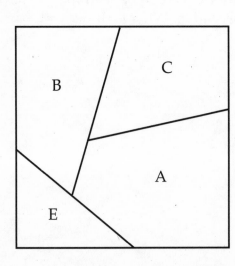

**6** Fascinate. The missing letters are A and T.

**7** B (axiom).

**8** Rest and wrest.

**9** A (0). The sum of each horizontal, vertical, and diagonal line equals 12.

**10** Set at ease.

**11** D.
The others contain only one small white circle, while this one has two.

**12** D (belfry).
The others are inside the main part of a church; the belfry is where the bells are.

**13** 375.
The previous number doubled, then at each stage 1, 2, 3, 4, 5, 6, and 7, respectively, is added.
1 + 1 + 1 = 3;
3 + 3 + 2 = 8;
8 + 8 + 3 = 19;
19 + 19 + 4 = 42;
42 + 42 + 5 = 89;
89 + 89 + 6 = 184;
184 + 184 + 7 = 375.

# Answers

**14** A (innocent).

**15** C (tangle).

**16** C.

**17** Long.

**18** Jujube.

**19** G. The others form identical pairs in different rotations: A&F, B&C, D&E.

**20** Zephyr (a wind).

**21** C.
Different symbols in adjoining circles on the same row are carried into the circle between them in the row above. Similar symbols in the same place are dropped.

**22** E (energetic).

**23** D (spurious, which means false). The others mean irregular or unreliable.

**24** 67.
The order of numbers reverses and the lowest digit is dropped.

**25** Bagatelle.

**26** Maniacal.
The missing letters are M and I.

**27** D.

**28** Cloudiness.

**29** A (a mixture).

**30** Yashmaks.
The missing letters are Y and M.

# Test Nine

Four of the five pieces below can be fitted together to form a decagon. Which is the odd one out?

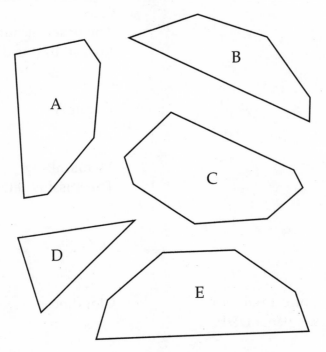

Which of the circles, A, B, C, D, or E, should replace the question mark below?

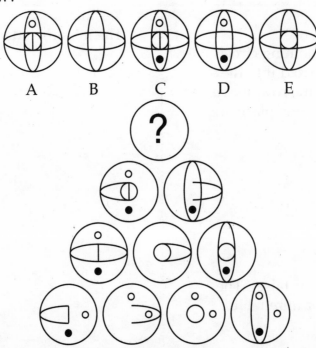

If the missing letters in the two circles below are correctly inserted they will form synonymous words. The words are read in a clockwise direction, and the letters are consecutive. What are the words and missing letters?

A chandler collected candle ends until he had 2197. How many candles in total could he make and burn from these if 13 candles ends make up one candle, and these ends are collected and reused?

**WAVE : GESTICULATE**

Which pair of words below have the same relationship as the words above?

**A. RUN : SAUNTER**
**B. KICK : GENUFLECT**
**C. SNORE : ANNOY**
**D. LAUGH : CHANT**
**E. WINK : NICTITATE**

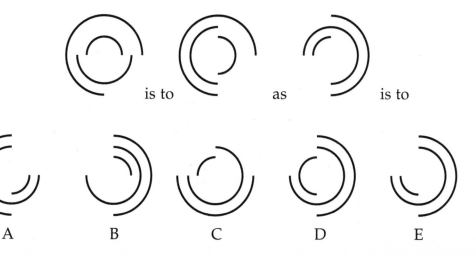

**7**

What number is missing from the third column?

18 24 54

15 40 15

6 3 ?

**8**

What two words are antonymous?

A. SALUBRIOUS
B. FRETTING
C. WORRIED
D. BUSY
E. STRONG
F. MORBID

**9**

What is the odd one out?

A. HOLE
B. ICE
C. ELEPHANT
D. LEG
E. SEA

**10**

4986 : 1314 : 45

What series has the same relationship as the one above?

A. 2386 : 1314 : 45
B. 7842 : 1513 : 64
C. 7217 : 1862 : 34
D. 9875 : 1217 : 83
E. 8795 : 1514 : 65

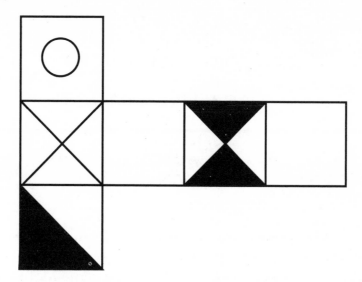

When the above is folded to form a cube, one of the figures below can be produced. What is it?

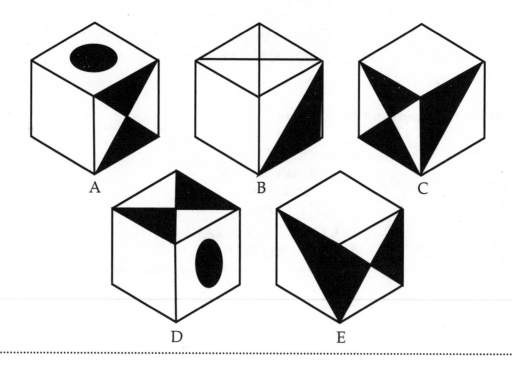

A  B  C

D  E

KNIFE is to CUT as CLEAVER is to?

       **A. SEVER**
    **B. LACERATE**
      **C. CHOP**
      **D. SLICE**
    **E. IMPALE**

**13**

What word goes with:

**AGE   PORT   ABLE   WORD**

A. LIKE
B. OVER
C. KIND
D. ARM
E. MAN

**14**

In a game of 12 players that lasts for exactly 75 minutes there are six reserves who alternate equally with starting players. It means that all players, including reserves, are in the game for exactly the same amount of time. How long is this?

A. 30 MINUTES
B. 40 MINUTES
C. 50 MINUTES
D. 55 MINUTES
E. 60 MINUTES

**15**

What two words are synonymous?

A. NOISY
B. WORTHY
C. LOWLY
D. LAUDABLE
E. COMPLIMENTARY
F. FROTHY

**16**

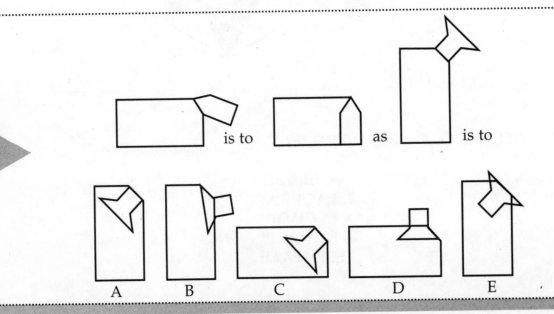

**17**

What is the group noun for a number of LEOPARDS?

A. CHIP
B. HUNT
C. STRIDE
D. PACK
E. LEAP

**18**

What two words are synonymous?

A. JAUNT
B. JUMP
C. INSULT
D. OUTING
E. PROMISE
F. IMAGINE

**19**

Place two three-letter segments together to form an extinct animal.

MBO   STU   AFE   GGA   GIR   QUA

**20**

If the missing letters in the circle below are correctly inserted they will form an eight-letter word. The word will not have to be read in a clockwise direction, but the letters are consecutive. What is the word and missing letters?

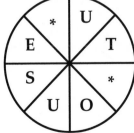

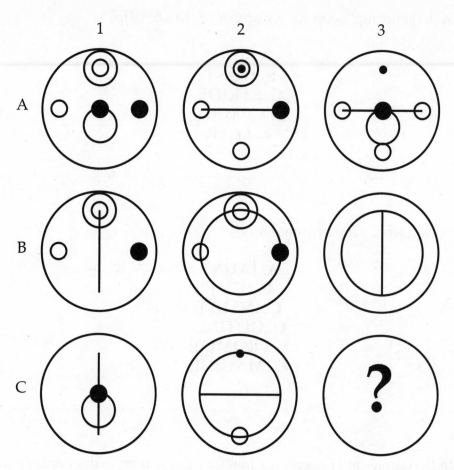

Which of the circles below should replace the question mark above?

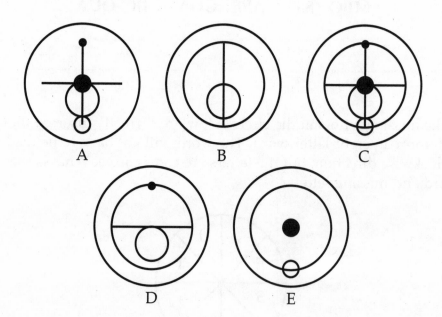

If the missing letters in the two circles below are correctly inserted they will form synonymous words. The words do not have to be read in a clockwise direction, but the letters are consecutive. What are the words and missing letters?

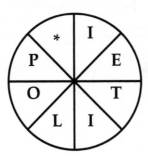 

A word can be placed in the brackets that has the same meaning as the words outside. What is it? Each dot represents a letter.

**TREE  ( • • • • )  YEARN**

Find a six-letter word made up of only the following four letters?

**S H**
**A R**

What word is an antonym of LIEGE?

**A. LORD**
**B. VASSAL**
**C. SOVEREIGN**
**D. FORTRESS**
**E. NUNCIO**

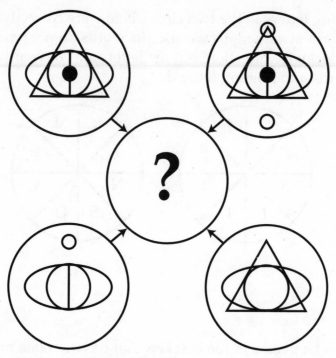

Each line and symbol that appears in the four outer circles, above, is transferred to the middle circle according to how many times it appears, as follows:

**One time — it is transferred**
**Two times — it is possibly transferred**
**Three times — it is transferred**
**Four times — it is not transferred**

Which of the options below should appear as the middle circle?

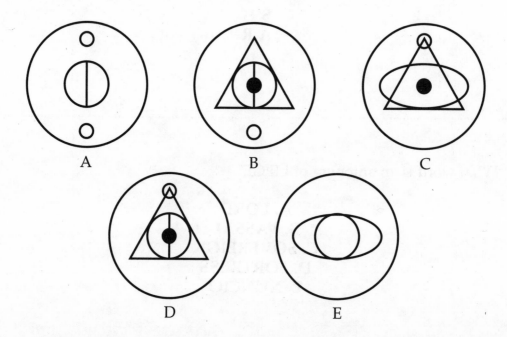

**27**

What word is a synonym of NUBILE?

**A. LITHE**
**B. MARRIAGEABLE**
**C. INEBRIATED**
**D. LISSOM**
**E. SUPPLE**

**28**

What word can be placed in front of the other five to form five new words or phrases? Each dot represents a letter.

( • • • • )

BALL
WAY
LAND
FLIER
BROW

**29**

If the missing letter in the circle below is correctly inserted it will form an eight-letter word. The word will not have to be read in a clockwise direction, but the letters are consecutive. What is the word and missing letter?

**30**

What is a SHADOOF?

**A. A SHADOWY FIGURE**
**B. A RESERVOIR**
**C. A DAM**
**D. A WATER-RAISING CONTRAPTION**
**E. A RUNNING STREAM**

# Answers

**1** B.

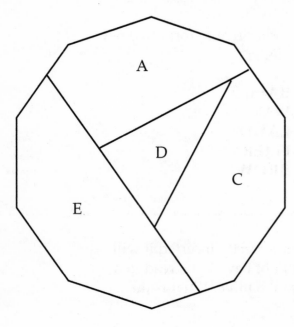

**2** A.
Different symbols in adjoining circles on the same row are carried into the circle between them in the row above. Similar symbols in the same place are dropped.

**3** Standard and ordinary. The missing letters are N and D (standard) and D and Y (ordinary).

**4** 183. 2197 ÷ 13 = 169.
The 169 candle stubs can be reused, so 169 ÷ 13 = 13 and 13 ÷ 13 = 1.
Therefore 169 + 13 + 1 = 183.

**5** E (wink : nictitate).

**6** B.
The two innermost segments both rotate 90° clockwise.

**7** 18.
In each column (top ÷ bottom) x 5 = middle. (54 ÷ 18) [3] x 5 = 15.
Others are (18 ÷ 6) [3] x 5 =15; (24 ÷ 3) [8] x 5 = 40.

**8** A (salubrious) and F (morbid).

**9** Elephant. The others can all be prefixed by black; elephant can only be prefixed by white.

**10** E (8795 : 1514 : 65).
The sum of the first two digits and the sum of the last two digits are put together and the process is repeated.

**11** A.

**12** C (chop).
A cleaver chops as a knife cuts.

142

# Answers

**13** ▶ B (over).
All the words can be prefixed by pass to make new words.

**14** ▶ C (50 minutes).
The game lasts 75 minutes and 12 players can be in the game for its duration, so there are a total of 900 player minutes (75 minutes x 12 players)  If 18 players are involved, the sum is (75 x 12) [900] ÷ 18 = 50.

**15** ▶ B (worthy) and D (laudable).

**16** ▶ A.
The top figure is folded along its adjoining line and moves into the lower one.

**17** ▶ E (lepe).

**18** ▶ A (jaunt) and D (outing).

**19** ▶ Quagga.

**20** ▶ Outhouse.
The missing letters are O and H.

**21** ▶ C.
Reading across columns and down rows, unique elements in the first two are transferred to the third (bottom or right). Common elements disappear.

**22** ▶ Impolite and insolent.
The missing letters are M (impolite) and L and T (insolent).

**23** ▶ Pine.

**24** ▶ Harass.

**25** ▶ B (vassal).

**26** ▶ B.

**27** ▶ B (marriageable).

**28** ▶ High.

**29** ▶ Hireling.
The missing letter is H.

**30** ▶ D (a water-raising contraption).

Four of the five pieces below can be fitted together to form a perfect square. Which is the odd one out?

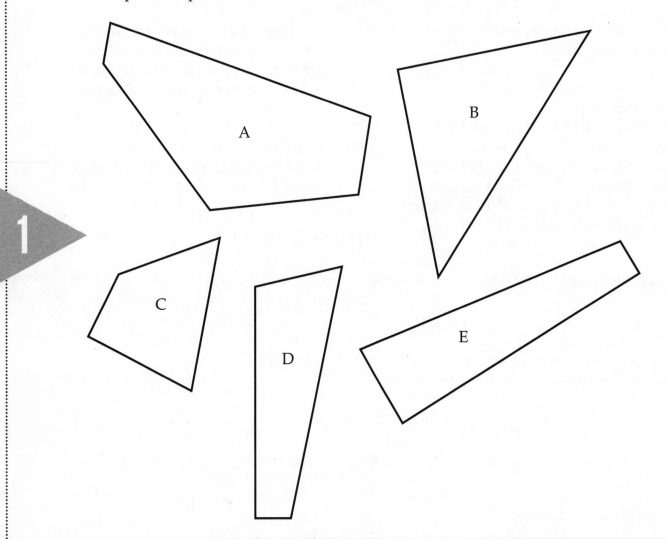

**1**

**PHILANDER : FLIRT**

Which pair of words below have the same relationship as the words above?

**2**

A. OBTAIN : FIND
B. MISTRUST : MISTREAT
C. PROSAIC : UNUSUAL
D. GREET : SALUTE
E. HUG : LOVE

**3**

Which of the following is not an anagram of a reptile?

A. ON CANADA
B. TIN ROOM
C. COOL CIDER
D. CAROB
E. BIT HAUL

**4**

What number is the odd one out?

A. 36119
B. 22515
C. 57624
D. 28918
E. 90030

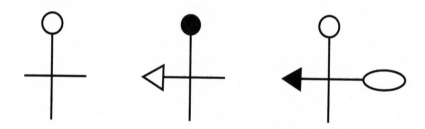

Which of the figures below will continue the sequence above?

**5**

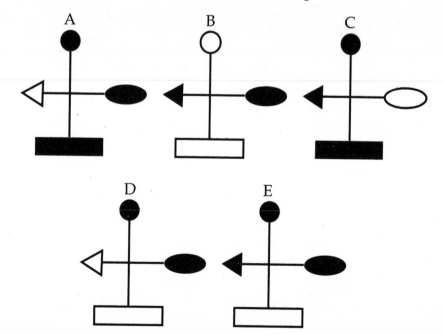

**6**

What words are antonymous?

A. CHANGE
B. ADMIRE
C. SOOTHE
D. STIR
E. VEX
F. EXPAND

**7**

Which of the following is the odd one out?

A. FEMUR
B. PATELLA
C. FIBULA
D. ULNA
E. TIBIA

**8**

What number should replace the question mark?

100   99.5   98.5   97   95   ?

**9**

Complete the two words using the letters of the following once only.

**IDLING TURN**

• A • • T • E •      • A • • T • E •

**10**

**CRISIS (PRAISE) SPREAD**

Following the same rules as above, what word should go in the brackets?

**REPOSE ( • • • • • • ) ARENAS**

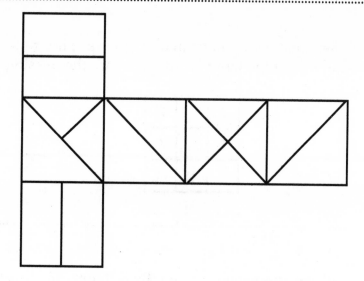

When the above is folded to form a cube, one of the figures below can be produced. What is it?

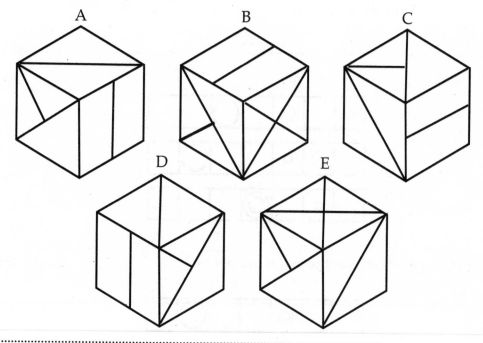

What number replaces the question mark?

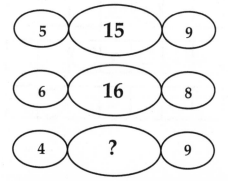

| 5 | 15 | 9 |
| 6 | 16 | 8 |
| 4 | ? | 9 |

**13**

Start at a corner square and move in a clockwise spiral to the middle to spell out a nine-letter word. What are the missing letters?

| E |   | H |
|---|---|---|
| F | T | E |
|   | R | A |

**14**

By 8.00 pm, all the guests had arrived. By 8.30 pm, one-third of them had left. By 9.30 pm, one-third of those remaining had also departed. By 11.00 pm, the same had happened again, and one-third of those remaining had gone. After this, only 16 guests remained. How many guests were at the party at 8.00 pm?

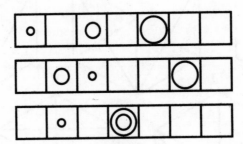

What should continue the sequence above?

**15**

A

B

C

D

E

**16**

Find a six-letter word made up of only the following four letters?

E L
T Y

**17**

What word can be placed in front of the other five to form five new words or phrases? Each dot represents a letter.

( • • • • • )

UP
TRIP
ABOUT
SHOULDERED
NUMBER

**18**

What number should replace the question mark?

119  108  99  81  72  ?

A. 63
B. 64
C. 65
D. 66
E. 67

**19**

If the missing letters in the circle below are correctly inserted they will form an eight-letter word. The word will not have to be read in a clockwise direction, but the letters are consecutive. What is the word and missing letters?

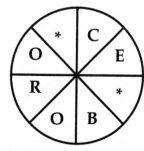

**20**

If 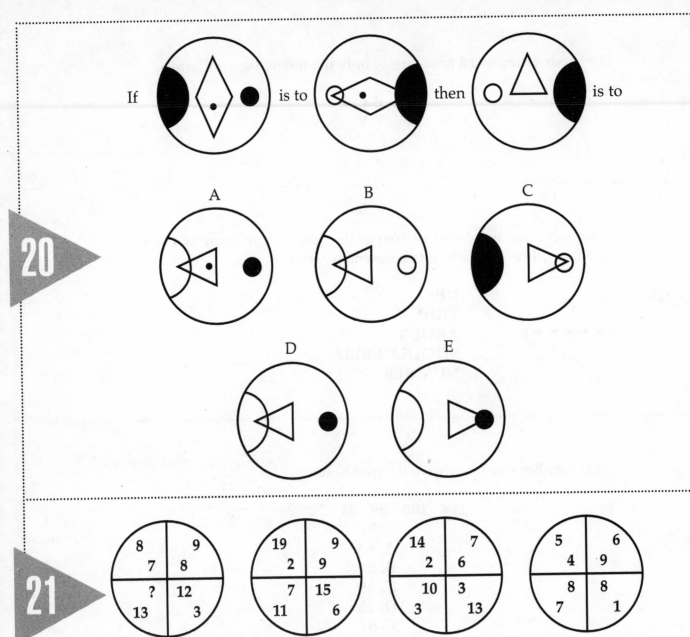 is to ⟨○──⟩ then ○△ is to

A   B   C

D   E

**21**

What number should replace the question mark?

**22**

If the missing letters in the two circles below are correctly inserted they will form synonymous words. The words do not have to be read in a clockwise direction, but the letters are consecutive. What are the words and missing letters?

**23**

A word can be placed in the brackets that has the same meaning as the words outside. What is it? Each dot represents a letter.

**HORSE STRAP ( • • • • • • • • • ) GAMBLING TERM**

**24**

Place two three-letter segments together to form a fish.

**ENT   LET   PIK   MUL   GER   PAR**

**25**

Which of the following is the odd one out?

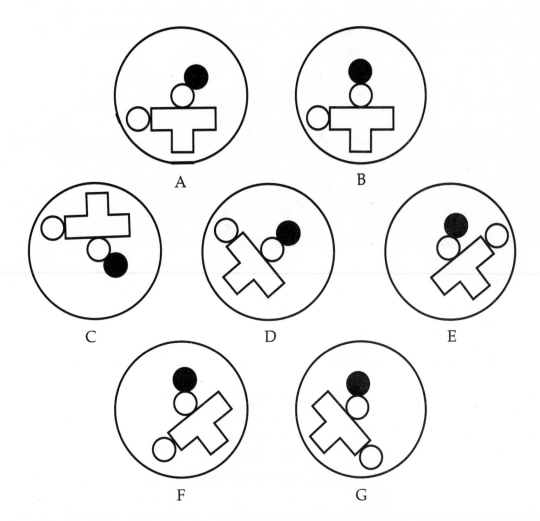

A          B

C          D          E

F          G

**26**

If one letter in each of the four words below is changed, a phrase can be found. What is it?

**SIN OF SHE HENCE**

**27**

Simplify the following and find the value of x.

$$\frac{5}{8} \div \frac{7}{16} \div \frac{10}{14} = x$$

**28**

If the missing letter in the circle below is correctly inserted it will form an eight-letter word. The word will not have to be read in a clockwise direction, but the letters are consecutive. What is the word and missing letter?

**29**

What word is a synonym of JOCOSE?

**A. MISERLY**
**B. MISERABLE**
**C. COMICAL**
**D. GENEROUS**
**E. IMPARTIAL**

Which of the hexagons at the bottom should replace the question mark below?

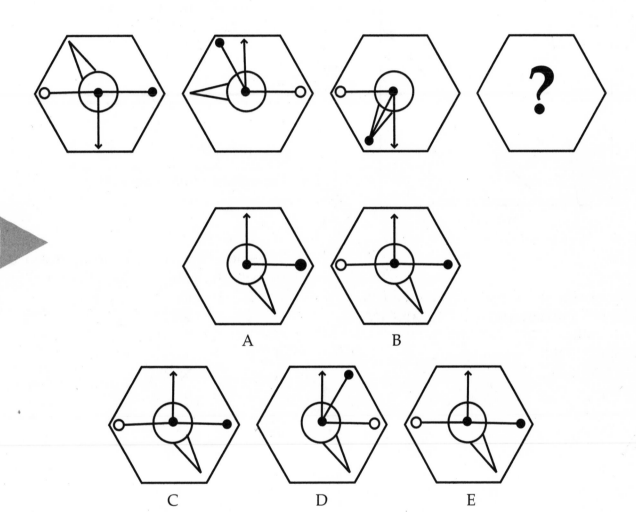

A

B

C

D

E

# Answers

**1** D.

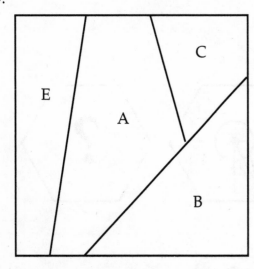

**2** D (greet : salute).

**3** E (bit haul) which makes halibut, a fish. The other anagrams are: ON CANADA (anaconda), TIN ROOM (monitor), COOL CIDER (crocodile), and CAROB (cobra).

**4** D (28918).
The first three digits of the other numbers is the square of the last two digits: 361 is the square of 19, 225 is the square of 15, 576 is the square of 24, and 900 is the square of 30.

**5** D.
A new and different white symbol is added to one of the arms at each stage. The symbol then alternates between black and white at each stage.

**6** C (soothe) and E (vex).

**7** D (ulna, a bone in a human's arm). The others are bones in a human's leg.

**8** 92.5.
At each stage the numbers reduce by 0.5, 1, 1.5, 2, and 2.5, respectively.

**9** Gauntlet and daintier.

**10** 10.  Reason.
Three letters of the left and right words transfer to the middle as follows:

```
R   E   P   O   S   E
    2       5   4
(R   E   A   S   O   N)
 1   2   3   4   5   6
A   R   E   N   A   S
1       6   3
```

**11** D.

**12** 12. In each case the sum is (left x right) ÷ 3 = middle. (4 x 9) [36] ÷ 3 = 12. The others are: (5 x 9) [45] ÷ 3 = 15; (6 x 8) [48] ÷ 3 = 16.

**13** Heartfelt.
The missing letters are T and L.

**14** 54 guests at 8.00 pm.

# Answers

**15** ▶ D.
At each stage, the small circle moves two squares right and one left; the medium circle moves one left and two right; and the large circle moves one right and two left.

**16** ▶ Eyelet.

**17** ▶ Round.

**18** ▶ A (63). The sum of digits is removed from the first number to create the second and the sequence continues.
72 – 7 – 2 = 63. The sequence starts:
119 – 1 – 1 – 9 = 108;
108 – 1 – 8 = 99;
99 – 9 – 9 = 81;
81 – 8 – 1 = 72.

**19** ▶ Objector.
The missing letters are J and T.

**20** ▶ E.
The middle figure rotates 90° clockwise and the outer figures rotate 180° and change from black to white and vice versa.

**21** ▶ 4.
In each case the sums of numbers diagonally opposite sectors are the same.

**22** ▶ Increase and heighten. The missing letters are C and S (increase) and H twice (heighten).

**23** ▶ Martingale.

**24** ▶ Mullet.

**25** ▶ E.
The others all have identical pairs in different rotations: A and F, B and D, and C and G.

**26** ▶ Sit on the fence.

**27** ▶ 2.
The sum can expressed as: $\frac{5}{8} \times \frac{16}{7} \times \frac{14}{10} = 2$.

**28** ▶ Guidance.
The missing letters are G and N.

**29** ▶ C (comical).

**30** ▶ A. In each case, the white circle and black arrow both rotate 180°, the white arrow rotates 60° anti- (counter) clockwise, and the black dot rotates 120° anti- (counter) clockwise.

Which three of the five pieces below can be fitted together to form a cuboid?

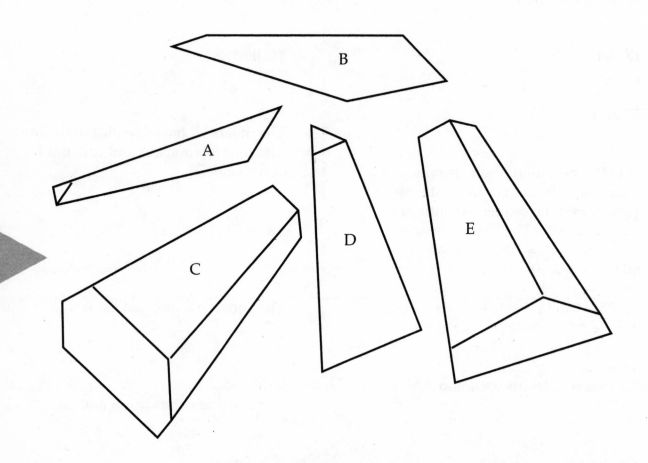

1

A. ACD
B. ABC
C. CDE
D. BCD
E. ADE

**2**

Find the starting point and move from square to adjoining square, horizontally or vertically, but not diagonally, to spell a 12-letter word, using each letter once only. What are the missing letters?

| R | A |   |
|---|---|---|
|   | A | M |
| S | S | E |
| I | N |   |

**3**

What number should replace the question mark?

**53 (3) 59**
**71 (9) 79**
**29 (?) 98**

**4**

THREE MEN EXIT is an anagram of a three-word phrase that could also be "the highest degree". What is the phrase?

**5**

Find two words with different spellings, but sound alike, that can mean:

**SCREEN / HURRIED**

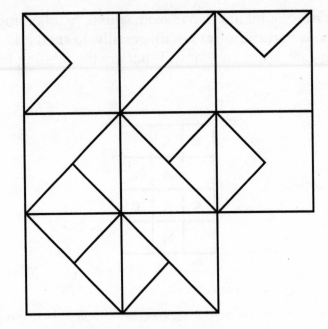

## 6

Which of the squares below will go in the blank space above?

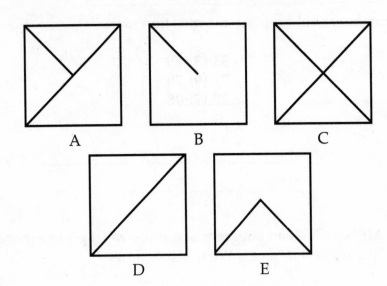

A          B          C

D          E

What number should replace the question mark?

**3   9   11   33   35   ?**

**8**

What two words are antonymous?

> **A. REFRESHING**
> **B. INVITING**
> **C. KIND**
> **D. SENSIBLE**
> **E. WISE**
> **F. INVIDIOUS**

**9**

A word can be placed in the brackets that has the same meaning as the words outside. What is it? Each dot represents a letter.

**GREEK GODDESS ( • • • • ) PONDER**

**10**

OUCH is to BROOCH as TORQUE is to?

> **A. CROWN**
> **B. NECKCHAIN**
> **C. HEADBAND**
> **D. EARRING**
> **E. RING**

**11**

What two words are synonymous?

> **A. BAN**
> **B. BANAL**
> **C. FIT**
> **D. HOLD**
> **E. PERMIT**
> **F. PROSCRIBE**

What positive number replaces the question mark?

| 2 | 4 | 2 |
|---|---|---|
| 16 | 12 | 48 |
| 8 | 12 | ? |

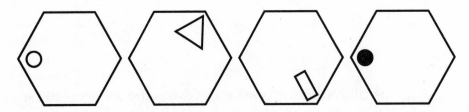

Which of the hexagons below will continue the above sequence?

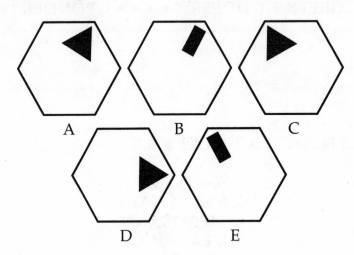

A          B          C

D          E

What number replaces the question mark?

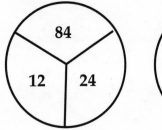

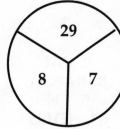

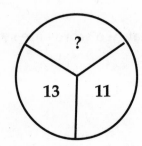

160

**15**

What word is the odd one out?

A. VARIETY
B. SPECIES
C. BREED
D. STOCK
E. STRAIN

**16**

What is the essential ingredient of SAUERKRAUT?

A. PEPPERS
B. CHEESE
C. SQUID
D. SAUSAGE
E. CABBAGE

**17**

Find a six-letter word made up of only the following four letters?

L B
P E

**18**

What word can be placed in front of the other five to form five new words? Each dot represents a letter.

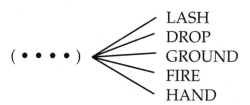

( • • • • )  LASH
DROP
GROUND
FIRE
HAND

If the missing letters in the circle below are correctly inserted they will form an eight-letter word. The word will not have to be read in a clockwise direction, but the letters are consecutive. What is the word and missing letters?

Which of the following is the odd one out?

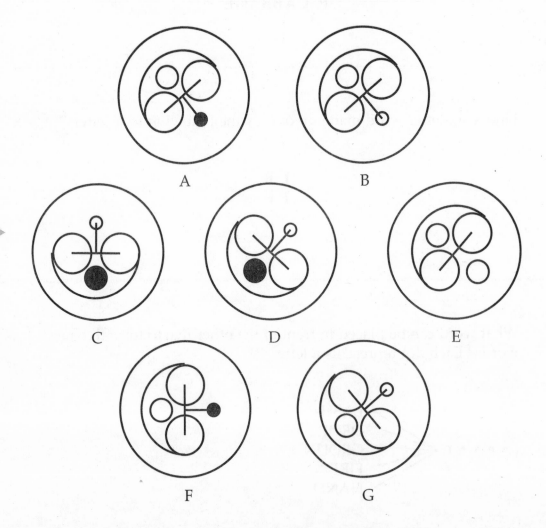

A

B

C

D

E

F

G

**21**

What word has the same meaning as ECLAT?

A. JEALOUSY
B. SORDID
C. PATIENCE
D. MYSTERY
E. APPLAUSE

**22**

If the missing letters in the two circles below are correctly inserted they will form synonymous words. The words do not have to be read in a clockwise direction, but the letters are consecutive. What are the words and missing letters?

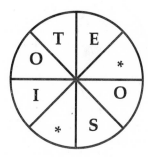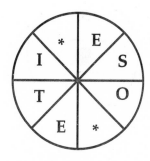

**23**

Place two three-letter segments together to form a nautical item.

SER   FUN   GUN   VAN   ELS   HAW

**24**

A word can be placed in the brackets that has the same meaning as the words outside. What is it? Each dot represents a letter.

MOVE ON ITS AXIS ( • • • ) COOKING UTENSIL

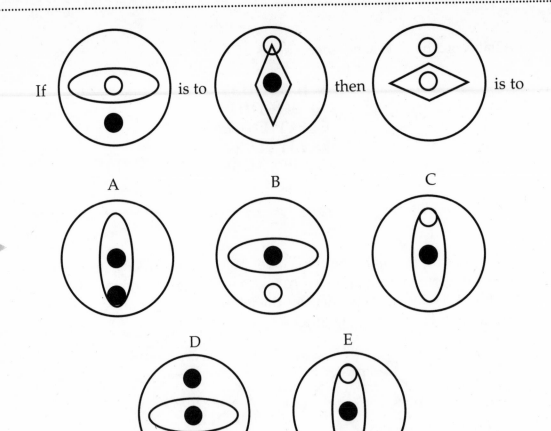

**25**

If [figure] is to [figure] then [figure] is to

A  B  C

D  E

**26**

What is the difference between the lowest cube number and the highest square number?

| 10 | 17 | 80 | 41 |
|----|----|----|----|
| 36 | 1  | 10 | 26 |
| 25 | 14 | 7  | 8  |
| 19 | 11 | 190| 23 |

**27**

What is the group noun for a number of OWLS?

A. GAGGLE
B. FLOCK
C. PARLIAMENT
D. MURMURATION
E. FLIGHT

**28**

What is a synonym of GENUFLECT?

A. ACCENTUATE
B. BREATHE HEAVILY
C. GIVE WAY
D. CLEAR THE THROAT
E. BEND THE KNEE

**29**

Which two words are antonymous?

A. ENTANGLE
B. COVERT
C. ASSUAGE
D. IRRITATE
E. BRANDISH

**30**

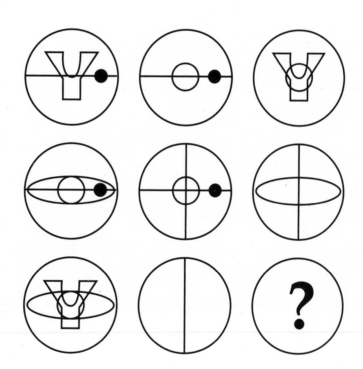

Which of the circles above should replace the question mark below?

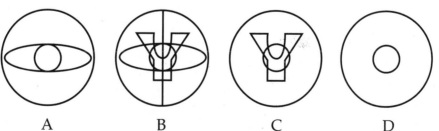

A       B       C       D

# Answers

**1** A (ACD).

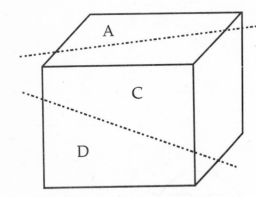

**2** Embarrassing.
The missing letters are, reading from top to bottom, B, R and G.

**3** 4.
The sums are: (right digits multiplied) ÷ (left digits multiplied) = middle. (9 x 8) [72] ÷ (2 x 9) [18] = 4.
The others are:
(5 x 9) [45] ÷ (5 x 3) [15] = 3;
(7 x 9) [63] ÷ (7 x 1) [7] = 9.

**4** In the extreme.

**5** Hide and hied.

**6** D.
Reading across columns and down rows, unique elements in the first two squares are transferred to the third (bottom or right). Common elements disappear.

**7** 105.
The sequence alternates:
x3, +2. 3 x 3 = 9;
9 + 2 = 11; 11 x 3 = 33;
33 + 2 = 35; 35 x 3 = 105.

**8** C (kind) and F (invidious).

**9** Muse.

**10** B (neckchain).

**11** A (ban) and F (proscribe).

**12** 24.
In each row (left x middle) ÷ 4 = right.
(8 x 12) [96] ÷ 4 = 24.
The others are: (2 x 4) [8] ÷ 4 = 2; (16 x 12) [192] ÷ 4 = 48.

**13** A.
The figures rotate 120° clockwise and the circle, triangle, and rectangle are white first time, black second time.

**14** 46.
The sums are: (top – left) ÷ 3 = right.
(46 – 13) [33] ÷ 3 = 11.
The others are:
(84 – 12) [72] ÷ 3 = 24;
(29 – 8) [21] ÷ 3 = 7.

# Answers

15 ▶ B (species, a general word).
The others are types of species.

16 ▶ E (cabbage).

17 ▶ Pebble.

18 ▶ Back.

19 ▶ Outshone.
The missing letters are O and H.

20 ▶ E. The others are all pairs in different rotations, A and F, B and G, and C and D.

21 ▶ E (applause).

22 ▶ Toilsome and tiresome.
The missing letters are L and M (toilsome) and R and M (tiresome).

23 ▶ Hawser.

24 ▶ Pan.

25 ▶ A.
The oval becomes a diamond and vice versa, and rotates 90° clockwise. The circles change from black to white and vice versa, and rotate 180°.

26 ▶ 28.
The lowest cube number is 8, the highest square number is 36; 36 − 8 = 28.

27 ▶ C (parliament).

28 ▶ E (bend the knee).

29 ▶ C and D (assuage and irritate).

30 ▶ B.
Reading across columns and down rows, unique elements in the first two circles are transferred to the third (bottom or right). Common elements disappear.

# Test Twelve

Which three of the five pieces below can be fitted together to form a perfect square?

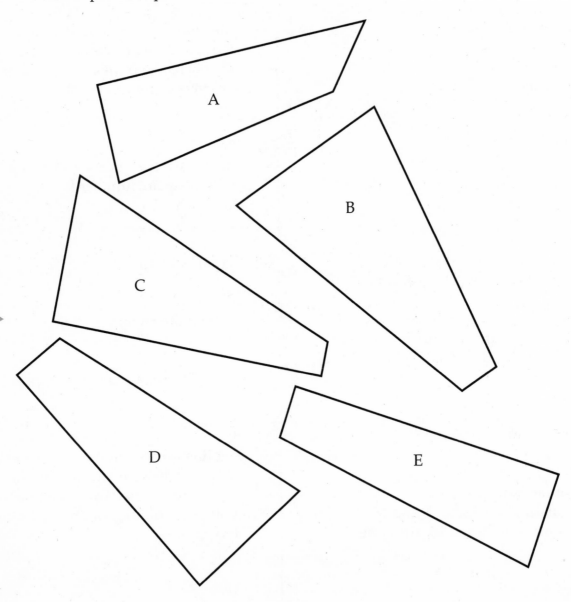

A. ABC
B. BDE
C. BCD
D. ADE
E. ACD

What option below continues the above sequence?

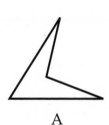  

A        B        C        D        E

**3**

A three-word phrase, below, has had each word's initial letter removed. What is the phrase?

**IRDFREY**

**4**

What number should replace the question mark?

0  1  5  14  30  ?

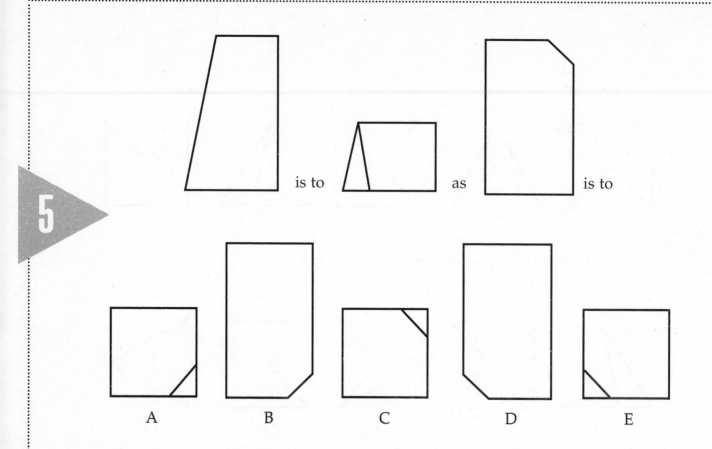

**5**

is to ... as ... is to

A    B    C    D    E

To which square from the five at the bottom can a dot be added so that it meets the same conditions as the box below?

**6**

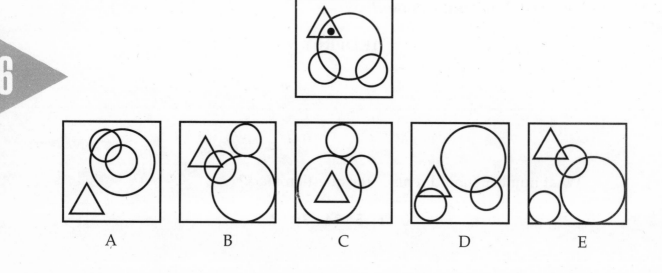

A    B    C    D    E

**7**

If one letter in each of the four words below is changed, a phrase can be found. What is it?

**TALE FAR I RUDE**

**8**

A train, 0.25m long, going at a speed of 40mph enters a tunnel that is 2.25m long. How long does it take for all of the train to pass through the tunnel from the moment the front enters it, to the moment the rear emerges?

**9**

Which of the following is the odd one out?

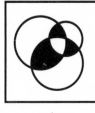
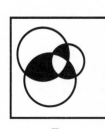
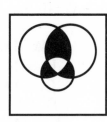
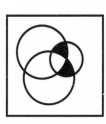

A          B          C          D

**10**

Start at a corner square and move in a clockwise spiral to the middle to spell out a nine-letter word. What are the missing letters?

| T | E | R |
|---|---|---|
|   | D | E |
| E |   | F |

**11**

Which of the following is not an anagram of a form of transport?

A. RAIL REIN
B. NOD GOAL
C. OLD PEAR
D. AIM LOO TUBE
E. CARVE FORTH

**12**

WIMBLE is to DRILL as ROUTER is to?

A. SAW
B. SHAPE
C. WRENCH
D. HIT
E. CUT

**13**

What word is a synonym of SALUTARY?

A. WELCOMING
B. SINGULAR
C. GLOWING
D. CRINGING
E. BENEFICIAL

**14**

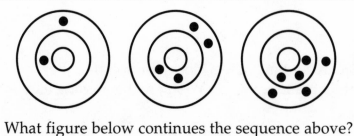

What figure below continues the sequence above?

A　　　　B　　　　C　　　　D　　　　E

**15**

What number replaces the question mark?

| 7 | 3 | 4 | 8 |
|---|---|---|---|
| 9 | 11 | ? | 5 |
| 6 | 9 | 4 | 1 |
| 4 | 1 | 1 | 4 |

**16**

If the missing letters in the two circles below are correctly inserted they will form synonymous words. The words do not have to be read in a clockwise direction, but the letters are consecutive. What are the words and missing letters?

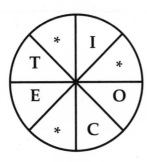 

**17**

Find a six-letter word made up of only the following four letters?

L B
F E

**18**

Place two three-letter segments to form a bird?

**RAN   LEW   ROW   TIT   CUR   SPA**

**19**

What word can be placed in front of the other five to form five new words? Each dot represents a letter.

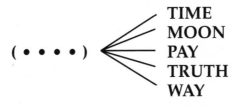

( • • • • )
TIME
MOON
PAY
TRUTH
WAY

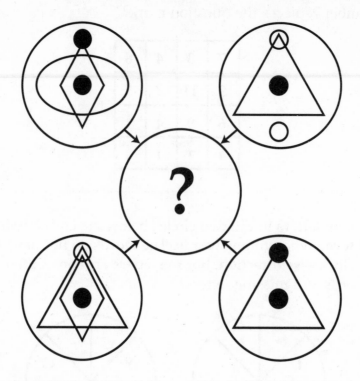

Each line and symbol that appears in the four outer circles, above, is transferred to the middle circle according to how many times it appears, as follows:

**One time — it is transferred**
**Two times — it is possibly transferred**
**Three times — it is transferred**
**Four times — it is not transferred**

Which of the circles below should appear in the middle circle?

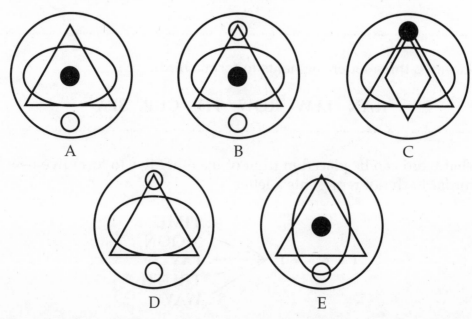

What number should replace the question mark?

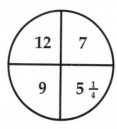 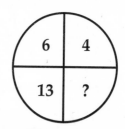

| 16 | 12 |
|----|----|
| 9 | $6\frac{3}{4}$ |

| 10 | 11 |
|----|----|
| 12 | $13\frac{1}{5}$ |

| 12 | 7 |
|----|----|
| 9 | $5\frac{1}{4}$ |

| 6 | 4 |
|----|----|
| 13 | ? |

If the missing letters in the circle below are correctly inserted they will form an eight-letter word. The word will not have to be read in a clockwise direction, but the letters are consecutive. What is the word and missing letters?

Which word is a synonym of SPINDRIFT?

**A. FLOTSAM**
**B. SEA-SPRAY**
**C. SPINNAKER**
**D. TOPSAIL**
**E. RUDDER-BEARING**

A word can be placed in the brackets that has the same meaning as the words outside. What is it? Each dot represents a letter.

**BASKET ( • • • • • • ) IMPEDE**

25

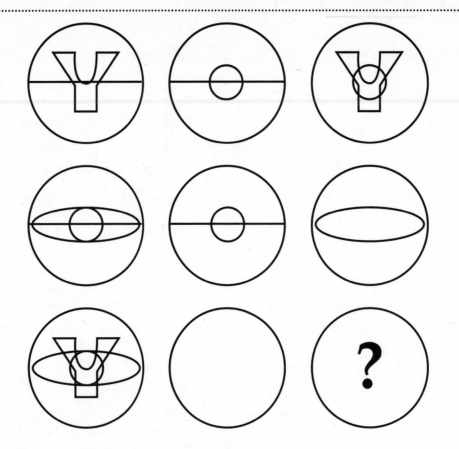

What circle should replace the question mark?

A B C D

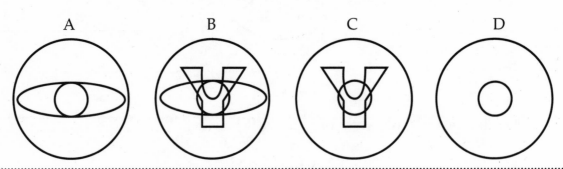

26

What is a CARBONADE?

**A. NECKWEAR**
**B. POACHER'S GUN**
**C. BEEF STEW**
**D. SOFT DRINK**
**E. BELT FOR BULLETS**

27

Place three two-letter segments together to form another word for falseness.

**DE MB SW UG IN HU DL**

**28**

What is the group noun for a number of PARTRIDGES?

A. COVEY
B. SEDGE
C. WEDGE
D. FLOCK
E. DRIFT

**29**

What word is a synonym of EXIGENCY?

A. INNUENDO
B. CIRCUITOUSLY
C. NECESSITY
D. DELUSION
E. DEVOUTNESS

**30**

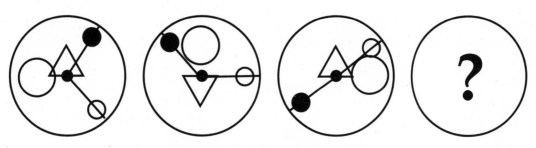

What circle will continue the sequence?

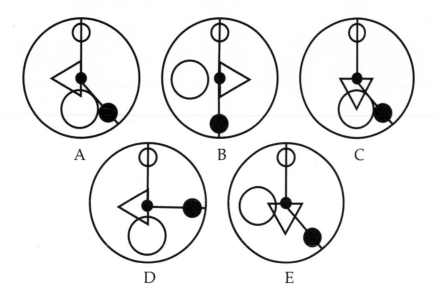

A          B          C

D          E

# Answers

**1**   B (BDE).

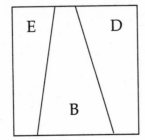

**2**   A.
There are alternate sequences, the right-angled figure rotates 90° clockwise, and the pointed figure rotates 120° clockwise.

**3**   Bird of prey.

**4**   55.
At each stage progressive square numbers are added. $0 + 1^2 (1) = 1$;
$1 + 2^2 (4) = 5$;
$5 + 3^2 (9)$ 14;
$14 + 4^2 (16) = 30$;
$30 + 5^2 (25) = 55$.

**5**   A.
The top half is folded across the middle and placed over the bottom half.

**6**   C.
The dot appears in the large circle and the triangle.

**7**   Take for a ride.

**8**   3 minutes, 45 seconds.
Add the train length (0.25m) to the tunnel length (2.25m) and multiply by the number of minutes per mile covered ($^{60}/_{40}$, or 1.5). 2.5 x 1.5 = 3.75.

**9**   D.
In the others all areas common to only two circles are shaded. In D, one such area is not covered.

**10**   Reflected.
The missing letters are L and C.

**11**   C (OLD PEAR or leopard).
The others are:
RAIL REIN (airliner),
NOD GOAL (gondola),
AIM LOO TUBE (automobile),
and CARVE FORTH (hovercraft).

**12**   E (cut).

**13**   E (beneficial).

**14**   C.
At each stage two dots are added; outer dots rotate 45° clockwise; inner dots rotate 45° anti- (counter) clockwise.

# Answers

7.
The sums are: (first column + third column) = (second column + fourth column). (9 + 7) = (11 + 5).
The others are:
(7 + 4) = (3 + 8);
(6 + 4) = (9 + 1);
(4 + 1) = (1 + 4).

Ricochet and bouncing.
The missing letters are C and H (ricochet) and B and N (bouncing).

Feeble.

Curlew.

Half.

D.

$8\frac{2}{3}$.
The sums are:
(bottom left x top right) = (top left x bottom right).
(13 x 4) [52] = (6 x $8\frac{2}{3}$) [52].
The others are:
(9 x 12) [108] x (16 x $6\frac{3}{4}$) [108];
(12 x 11) [132] = (10 x $13\frac{1}{5}$) [132];
(9 x 7) [63] x (12 x $5\frac{1}{4}$) [63].

Upstairs.
The missing letters are U and A.

B (sea-spray).

Hamper.

B.
Reading across columns and down rows, unique elements in the first two circles are transferred to the third (bottom or right). Common elements disappear.

C (beef stew).

Humbug.

A (covey).

C (necessity).

C.
At each stage the triangle rotates 180°, the large circle rotates 90° clockwise, the small white circle rotates 45° anti- (counter) clockwise, and the small black circle rotates 90° anti- (counter) clockwise.

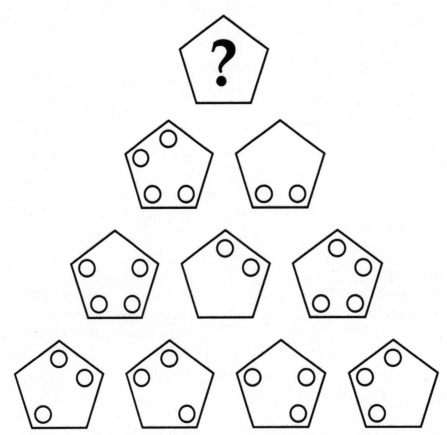

Which of the pentagons below should replace the question mark?

A     B     C     D     E

**1**

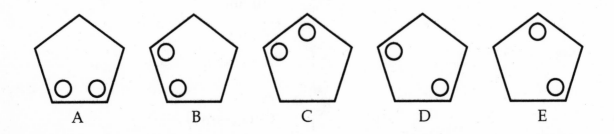

**2**

What word is a synonym of GENERIC?

> **A. PRECISE**
> **B. UNIVERSAL**
> **C. OLD**
> **D. WEAK**
> **E. COMPLETE**

Start at a corner square and move in a clockwise spiral to the middle to spell out a nine-letter word. What are the missing letters?

|   | O |   |
|---|---|---|
| A | L | A |
| C | I | N |

**4627 : 6445 : 8263**

Which series below has the same relationship as the series above?

**A. 5916 : 7734 : 9552**
**B. 4763 : 3854 : 2945**
**C. 1234 : 3214 : 4123**
**D. 7856 : 6947 : 4769**
**E. 2846 : 5971 : 8352**

EPIC PROSE is an anagram of what nine-letter word?

Which of the following pentagons in the odd one out?

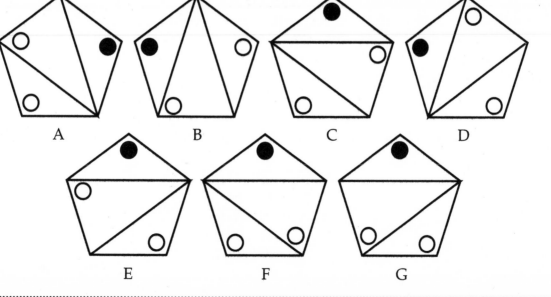

**7**

If one letter in each of the three words below is changed, a phrase can be found. What is it?

**ALL AS BASE**

**8**

Which of the following is the odd one out?

A. MOCHA
B. TAWNY
C. TEAL
D. UMBER
E. BEIGE

**9**

What two words are closest in meaning?

A. PURE
B. SORE
C. POUR
D. RAW
E. SAD
F. VILE

**10**

What word is an antonym of WOOLLY?

A. FLEXIBLE
B. REGULAR
C. PRECISE
D. RARE
E. NEBULOUS

**11**

EGGPLANT is to AUBERGINE as ZUCCHINI is to?

A. BREADFRUIT
B. SORREL
C. CAPSICUM
D. COURGETTE
E. ARTICHOKE

Which three of the five pieces below can be fitted together to form a perfect square?

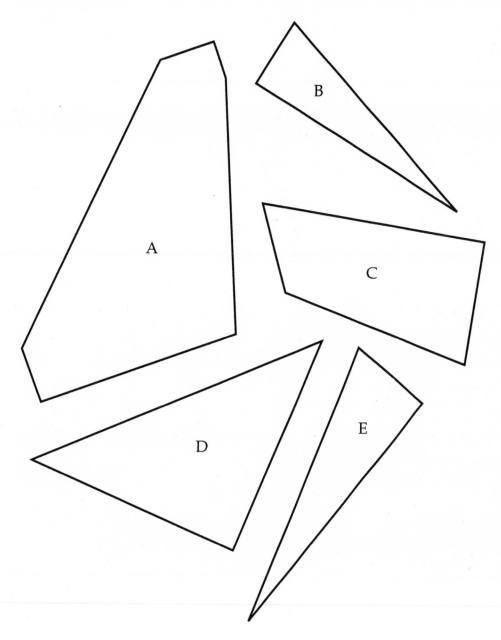

A. ABC
B. ABD
C. BCD
D. ADE
E. CDE

To which square at the bottom, A, B, C, D, or E, can a dot be
added so that it meets the conditions in the box above them?

**13**

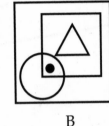

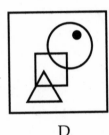

A        B        C        D        E

**14**

Find two words with different spellings, but sound alike,
that can mean:

**WAN / BUCKET**

What word goes with the following?

**RED   KING   TAN**

**A. LET**
**B. ROW**
**C. CAT**
**D. MAT**
**E. PAT**

**15**

**16**

Place three two-letter segments together to form a word for a system of magic.

**RO  OD  AS  VO  ST  OO  LO**

**17**

What number should replace the question mark?

**6  7  2  9  –2  11  ?**

**18**

A word can be placed in the brackets that has the same meaning as the words outside. What is it? Each dot represents a letter.

**POST ( • • • • • ) ANTE**

If the missing letters in the circle below are correctly inserted they will form an eight-letter word. The word will not have to be read in a clockwise direction, but the letters are consecutive. What is the word and missing letters?

**19**

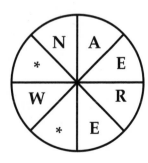

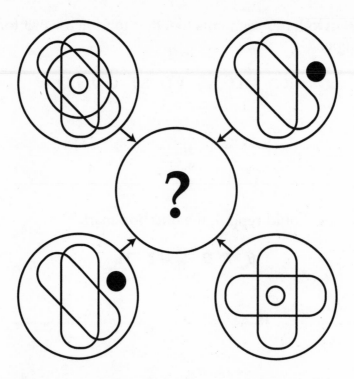

Each line and symbol that appears in the four outer circles, above, is transferred to the middle circle according to how many times it appears, as follows:

**One time — it is transferred**
**Two times — it is possibly transferred**
**Three times — it is transferred**
**Four times — it is not transferred**

Which of the circles below should appear as the middle circle?

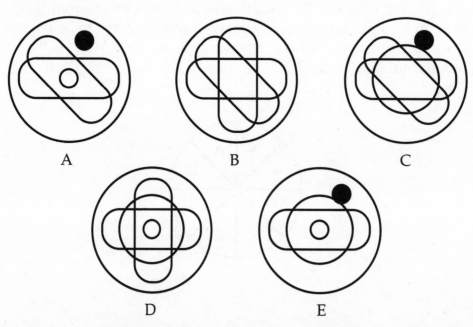

**21**

What two words are antonymous?

> **A. ANXIETY**
> **B. ARISTOCRACY**
> **C. PRELUDE**
> **D. CELEBRATED**
> **E. PROLETARIAT**

**22**

If the missing letters in the two circles below are correctly inserted they will form synonymous words. The words do not have to be read in a clockwise direction, but the letters are consecutive. What are the words and missing letters?

**23**

What word can be placed in front of the other five to form five new words? Each dot represents a letter.

$( \bullet \bullet \bullet )$ 
- NOT
- TEEN
- NON
- TON
- DID

**24**

Find a six-letter word made up of only the following four letters?

> H E
> C R

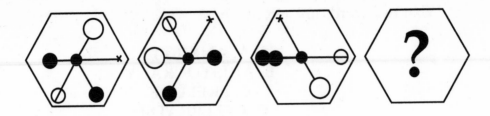

Which of the hexagons below should replace the question mark above?

A    B    C

D    E

---

What word is a synonym of FLACCID?

**A. TENUOUS**
**B. SPASMODIC**
**C. FLABBY**
**D. ROBUST**
**E. FASTIDIOUS**

---

Place two three-letter segments together to form a weapon.

**GEL   PIS   DAG   CUD   GEL   GIT**

---

What is the group noun given to a number of HERMITS?

**A. COLLECTION**
**B. CLAN**
**C. DWELLING**
**D. GATHERING**
**E. OBSERVANCE**

What word is the antonym of LACONIC?

**A. SENTENTIOUS**
**B. SUCCINCT**
**C. LOQUACIOUS**
**D. SCANTINESS**
**E. APPREHENSIVE**

Each of the nine squares in the grid marked 1A to 3C should incorporate all of the items which are shown in the squares of the same letter and number, at the left and top, respectively. For example, 2B should incorporate all of the symbols that are in squares 2 and B. One square, however, is incorrect. Which one is it?

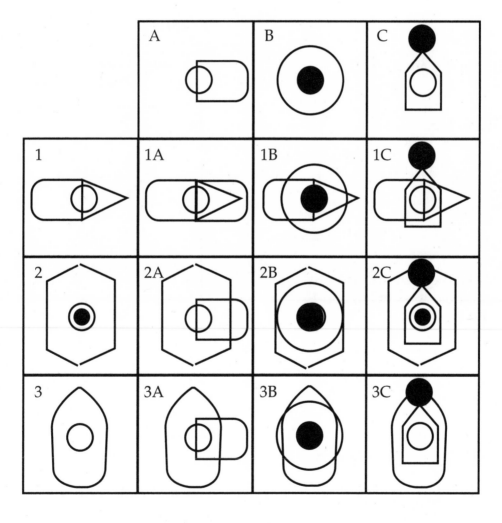

# Answers

**1**   C.
Differently positioned circles in adjoining pentagons on the same row are carried into the pentagon between them in the row above. Similarly positioned circles in the same place are dropped.

**2**   B (universal).

**3**   Botanical.
The missing letters are B and T.

**4**   A (5916 : 7734 : 9552).
At each stage add 1818.

**5**   Periscope.

**6**   F.
The others all have identical pairs in different rotations, A and G, B and E, and C and D.

**7**   Ill at ease.

**8**   C (teal, which is a shade of blue). The others are all brownish shades.

**9**   B (sore) and D (raw).

**10**   C (precise).

**11**   D (courgette).
It is another name for the vegetable.

**12**   B (ABD).

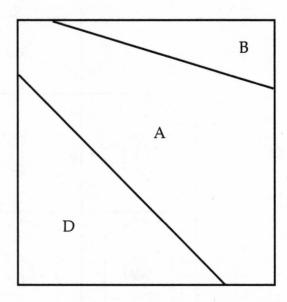

**13**   D.
The second dot appears in the link between the triangle and the square.

**14**   Pale and pail.

# Answers

**15** B (row).
The words can all be prefixed by SPAR, to make sparrow, sparred, sparking, spartan.

**16** Voodoo.

**17** –6.
There are alternate sequences, – 4 and + 2.
The series are: 6, 2, –2, and –6, and 7, 9, and 11.

**18** Stake.

**19** Anywhere. The missing letters are Y and H.

**20** C.

**21** B (aristocracy) and E (proletariat).

**22** Annoying and worrying. The missing letters are N and G (annoying) and W and Y (worrying).

**23** Can.

**24** Creche.

**25** A.
At each stage the short-lined black circle rotates 180°, the small white circle rotates 120° clockwise, the long-lined black circle rotates 60° clockwise, the large circle rotates 120° anti- (counter) clockwise, and the cross rotates 60° anti- (counter) clockwise.

**26** C (flabby).

**27** Cudgel.

**28** E (observance).

**29** C (loquacious).

**30** 2A.

**1**

Find two synonymous words in the inner and outer spirals of the circle below, one reading clockwise, the other anti- (counter) clockwise. What are the words and missing letters ?

**2**

Complete the two words using the letters of the following once only.

**FIND MRS BILGE**

• • S • E • • E •     • • S • E • • E •

**3**

What number should continue the sequence and replace the question mark?

**1 2 5 14 41 122 ?**

**4**

What word is an antonym of PSEUDO?

**A. NORMAL**
**B. ARTIFICIAL**
**C. PRUDENT**
**D. AUTHENTIC**
**E. PROVISION**

Which of the following in the odd one out?

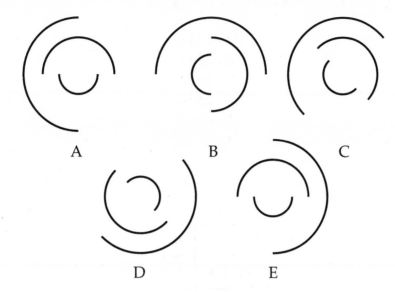

Which of the following is the odd one out?

**A. GOAT**
**B. BULL**
**C. CHICKEN**
**D. LION**
**E. RAM**

Complete the three-letter words which, reading down, will reveal an animal.

H E ( • )
F O ( • )
L E ( • )
S I ( • )
H A ( • )
A R ( • )
W O ( • )
B A ( • )

## 8

What number should replace the question mark?

**9768   7488   3744  ?**

A. 2516
B. 2732
C. 2814
D. 2816
E. 2852

| U |   | S |
|---|---|---|
| T | E | I |
| A | N |   |

Start at a corner square and move in a clockwise spiral to the middle to spell out a nine-letter word. What are the missing letters?

is to    as    is to

A      B      C      D      E

**11**

What word is a synonym of DISINTERESTED?

A. IMPARTIAL
B. STRONG
C. STAUNCH
D. IMPETURBABLE
E. ODD

**12**

EPISTLE : LETTER

Which pair of words below has the same relationship as the pair above?

A. HOMILY : FAREWELL
B. ACRONYM : OPPOSITE
C. LEXICON : ORIGIN
D. EPITHET : NAME
E. SYNTAX : REVENUE

**13**

SUDDEN MOMENT TUMULT WEANING

What comes next?

A. CHARMING
B. PRECIPITATION
C. THEME
D. HARMONY
E. CONGRATULATE

**14**

If one letter in each of the three words below is changed, a phrase can be found. What is it?

FIND ANY CANDY

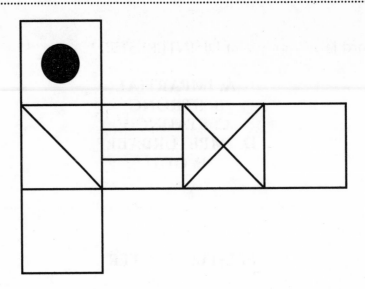

When the above is folded to form a cube, just one of the following can be produced. Which one is it?

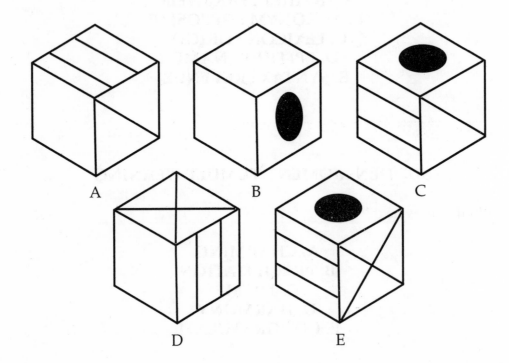

## 15

A

B

C

D

E

Find a six-letter word made up of only the following four letters?

V O
L E

What word can be placed in front of the other five to form five new words? Each dot represents a letter.

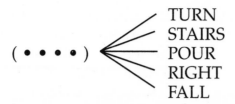

( • • • • ) < TURN
STAIRS
POUR
RIGHT
FALL

If the missing letters in the two circles below are correctly inserted they will form synonymous words. The words do not have to be read in a clockwise direction, but the letters are consecutive. What are the words and missing letters?

What two words are antonymous?

A. SPIRITUAL
B. POLLUTED
C. DEPRAVITY
D. CORPOREAL
E. HARMONY

Each of the nine squares in the grid marked 1A to 3C should incorporate all of the items which are shown in the squares of the same letter and number, at the left and top, respectively. For example, 2B should incorporate all of the symbols that are in squares 2 and B. One square, however, is incorrect.
Which one is it?

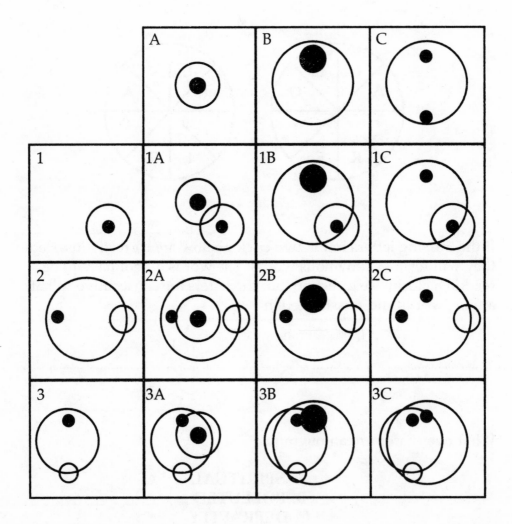

**21**

What word is a synonym of HUCKSTER?

        A. MECHANIC
        B. GAMBLER
        C. PEDLAR
        D. GIGOLO
        E. SEAMSTRESS

**22**

What number should replace the question mark?

**23**

Place two three-letter segments together to form a boat.

TER   MAS   GAL   IRE   CUT   EON

**24**

A word can be placed in the brackets that has the same meaning as the words outside. What is it? Each dot represents a letter.

DWELL ON CONSTANTLY ( • • • • ) MUSICAL INSTRUMENT

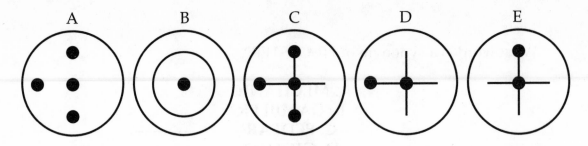

Which of the circles above should replace the question mark below?

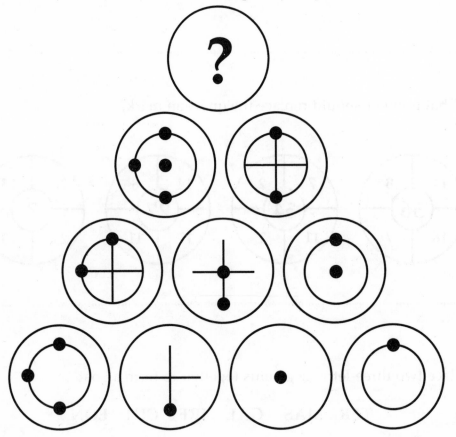

25

If the missing letters in the two circles below are correctly inserted they will form antonymous words. The words do not have to be read in a clockwise direction, but they are consecutive. What are the words and missing letters?

26

200

**27**

If the missing letters in the circle below are correctly inserted they will form an eight-letter word. The word will not have to be read in a clockwise direction, but the letters are consecutive. What is the word and missing letters?

N * Y P I * U A

**28**

What word is the odd one out?

A. GINKGO
B. JUNIPER
C. DEODAR
D. SISKIN
E. PAWPAW

**29**

What word is synonym of DIFFIDENT?

A. BASHFUL
B. DEMENTED
C. CELEBRATED
D. UNCOUTH
E. ILLICIT

**30**

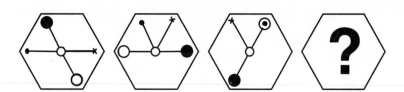

Which of the hexagons below should replace the question mark above?

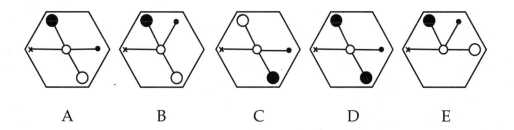

A          B          C          D          E

# Answers

**1** Opulence (outer ring) and richness (inner). the missing letters are P, L, and E (opulence) and S and H (richness).

**2** Disbelief and messenger.

**3** 365. At each stage multiply the previous number by three, then subtract one.
$1 \times 3 - 1 = 2$;
$2 \times 3 - 1 = 5$;
$5 \times 3 - 1 = 14$;
$14 \times 3 - 1 = 41$;
$41 \times 3 - 1 = 122$;
$122 \times 3 - 1 = 365$.

**4** D (authentic).

**5** E.
The others are the same figure in different rotations.

**6** C (chicken).
The others are all astrological signs (Capricorn – goat, Taurus – bull, Leo – lion, and Aries – ram).

**7** Reindeer. The words are:
heR, foE, leI, siN, haD, arE, woE, baR.

**8** A (2516). The first and third digits and second and fourth digits are made into two, two-digit numbers and multiplied together.
$96 \times 78 = 7488$;
$78 \times 48 = 3744$;
$34 \times 74 = 2516$.

**9** Signature. The missing letters are G and R.

**10** B. The circles in the two boxes are transferred to the third one only if they are not in similar positions. Similarly-placed circles disappear.

**11** A. Impartial.

**12** D (epithet : name).

**13** C (theme).
The initial letters of the words are the same as the days of the week.

**14** Fine and dandy.

**15** E.

**16** Evolve.

# Answers

**17** Down.

**18** Overhaul and overtake. The missing letters are V and H (overhaul) and V and K (overtake).

**19** A (spiritual) and D (corporeal).

**20** 2C.

**21** C (pedlar).

**22** 64. In each case the sum is (top left − bottom right) x (bottom left − top right). (26 − 18) [8] x (21 − 13) [8] = 64.

The others are:
(14 − 7) [7] x (16 − 8) [8] = 56;
(7 − 1) [6] x (11 − 2) [9] = 54;
(14 − 11) [3] x (17 − 8) [9] = 27.

**23** Cutter.

**24** Harp.

**25** D.
Different symbols in adjoining circles on the same row are carried into the circle between them in the row above. Similar symbols in the same place are dropped.

**26** Cheerful and desolate.
The missing letters are H and F (cheerful) and D and L (desolate).

**27** Piquancy.
The missing letters are Q and C.

**28** D (siskin, a bird).
The others are trees.

**29** A (bashful).

**30** A.
At each stage the large circles both rotate 120° clockwise, the dot rotates 60° clockwise, and the cross rotates 60° anti- (counter) clockwise.

# Test **Bonanza**

**1**

Place four of the three-letter segments together to form two synonymous words?

| HEW | INT | ETH | EST | ICS | NIC | ION |
|-----|-----|-----|-----|-----|-----|-----|
| ONE | HID | IVE | STR | MOT | NAT | ESC |

**2**

**AGLOW   ENVY   GHOST   HINT   ?**

Which one of the words below should replace the question mark above?

A. CALM
B. ANNOY
C. HOPE
D. FIST
E. MAKE

**3**

What number should replace the question mark?

**13  44  88  176  847  ?**

**4**

Which of the following words in the odd one out?

A. DULCET
B. SOFT
C. MELODIC
D. EUPHONIOUS
E. HARMONIOUS

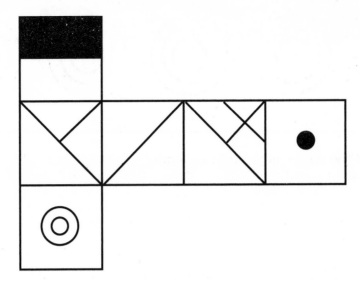

When the above is folded to form a cube, only one of the following can be produced. What one is it?

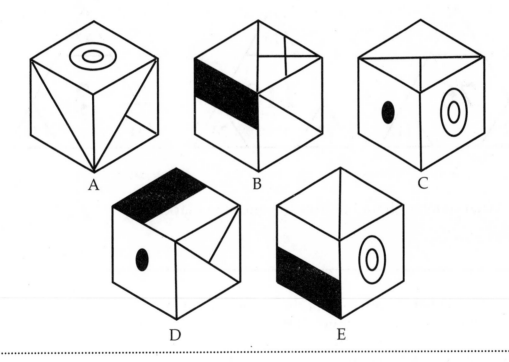

A
B
C
D
E

Find the starting point and move from square to adjoining square, horizontally or vertically, but not diagonally, to spell a 12-letter word, using each letter once only. What are the missing letters?

| I |   | U |
|---|---|---|
| N | A | L |
| A |   | I |
| M | E |   |

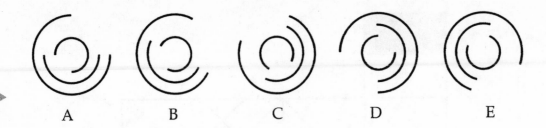

**7**

Which of the above is the odd one out?

**8**

DEMONIC VIPER is an anagram of what 12-letter word?

**9**

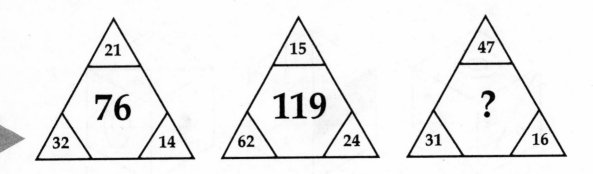

What number should replace the question mark?

**10**

Take one letter from each of the synonyms below, in order, to spell out another synonym of the keyword.

KEYWORD:    **VALOROUS**

SYNONYMS:    **STOUTHEARTED**
**FEARLESS**
**INTREPID**
**DOUGHTY**
**VALIANT**
**COURAGEOUS**

**11**

Which of the following words is the odd one out?

A. LARGE
B. BROAD
C. PERVASIVE
D. SWEEPING
E. WIDESPREAD

**12**

CLAVIER is to PIANO as TAMBOUR is to:

A. PERCUSSION
B. DRUM
C. XYLOPHONE
D. ACCORDION
E. WOODWIND

**13**

What number should replace the question mark?

1.5   0.5   3.5   10.5   7.5   2.5   ?

**14**

A word can be placed in the brackets to go at the end of the left word and the start of the right one, creating two new words. Each dot represents a letter. What are the three words?

OFF   (• • •)   ANGER

**15**

If a car had increased its average speed for a 180-mile journey by 5 mph, the journey would have been completed in 30 minutes less. What was the car's original average speed?

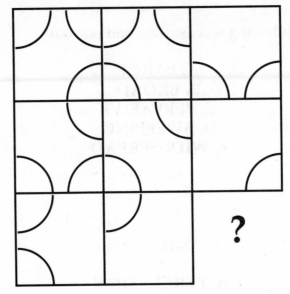

**?**

## 16

Which is of the squares below will replace the question mark above?

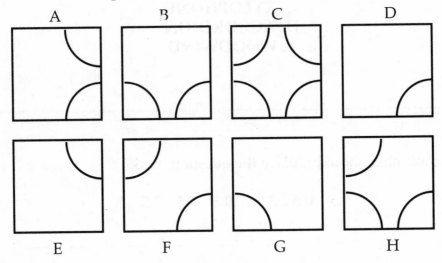

A    B    C    D

E    F    G    H

## 17

What two words are opposite in meaning?

**A. WORRIED**
**B. PIOUS**
**C. ANGRY**
**D. IRREVERENT**
**E. COVETOUS**
**F. DISTINGUISHED**

## 18

FOND MATES SALT JAM is an anagram of what three-word phrase that means wreckage?

What number in the grid below is two places away from itself multiplied by five, two places away from itself minus two, four places away from itself doubled, three places away from itself plus five, and two places away from itself divided by two.

| 13 | 46 | 12 | 16 | 20 | 38 |
| 23 | 16 | 6 | 24 | 22 | 8 |
| 3 | 7 | 4 | 1 | 30 | 9 |
| 4 | 2 | 50 | 40 | 8 | 76 |
| 15 | 90 | 6 | 18 | 2 | 11 |
| 10 | 14 | 5 | 8 | 20 | 28 |

A word can be placed in the brackets that has the same meaning as the words outside. What is it? Each dot represents a letter.

**OFTEN ( • • • • • • • ) HAUNT**

Which of the following words is opposite to REFINED?

**A. UNCOMFORTABLE**
**B. GAUCHE**
**C. BRITTLE**
**D. LOUD**
**E. ANNOYING**

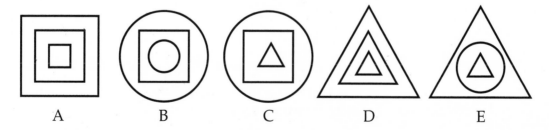

A       B       C       D       E

Which is the odd one out?

**23**

Complete the six-letter words so that the last two letters of one word are the first two of the next and the last two of the fifth word are the first two of the first.

```
( • • )  M  O  ( • • )
( • • )  R  I  ( • • )
( • • )  S  I  ( • • )
( • • )  V  I  ( • • )
( • • )  T  H  ( • • )
```

**24**

Which of the following has the same meaning as SUPPLICATION?

A. OVERNIGHT
B. REQUEST
C. ADDITION
D. MOVEMENT
E. CONFIRMATION

**25**

Find two synonymous words in the inner and outer spirals of the circle below, one reading clockwise, the other anti- (counter) clockwise. What are the words and missing letters ?

**26**

What is the meaning of an OREAD?

A. A MOUNTAIN NYMPH
B. A PRECIPICE
C. A PLAIN
D. A CLOCK
E. AN OBSERVATORY

**27** What is the decimal value of x in the following sum:

$$^7/_8 + ^7/_{12} - ^5/_6 = x$$

**28** Which of the following anagrams is not a BIRD?

A. LIGWATA
B. KYSRLAK
C. RAWSOPR
D. KITRALT
E. GONEDUD

**29** MENU MASCOT is an anagram of what 10-letter word?

**30**

Which of the circles below should replace the question mark above?

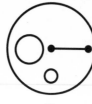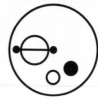

A          B          C          D          E

**31** Which two words are the closest in meaning?

A. MASQUERADE
B. MAUNDER
C. MAUDLIN
D. MEANDER
E. MEDIATE
F. MOODY

**32**

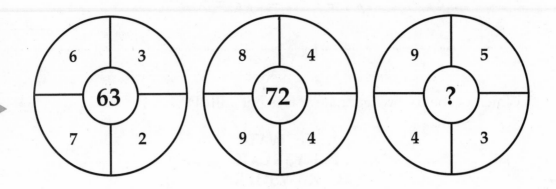

What number should replace the question mark?

**33**

What is the name given to a group of KNAVES?

A. BAND
B. DECEIT
C. RAYFUL
D. SESSION
E. THRONG

**34**

Which of the following is not a drink?

A. ANISETTE
B. FLUMMERY
C. MUSCATEL
D. EGG NOG
E. GRENADINE

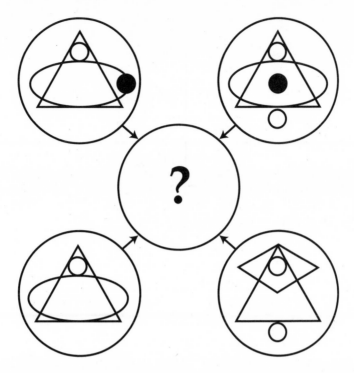

Each line and symbol that appears in the four outer circles, above, is transferred to the middle circle according to how many times it appears, as follows:

**One time — it is transferred**
**Two times — it is possibly transferred**
**Three times — it is transferred**
**Four times — it is not transferred**

Which of the circles below should appear as the middle circle?

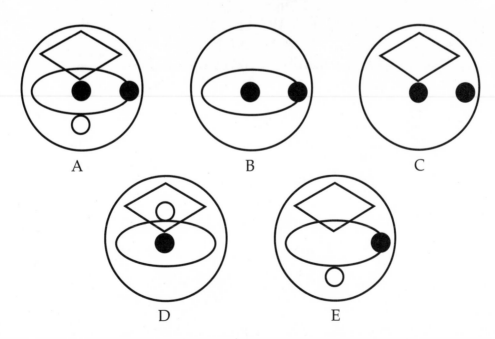

**36**

What number should replace the question mark?

**37**

A word can be placed in the brackets that has the same meaning as the words outside. What is it? Each dot represents a letter.

**TREE ( • • • • • • ) COUNTRY**

**38**

What is a PILAFF?

A. A TURKISH DISH
B. A WEAPON
C. A DANCE
D. A SKATING MOVEMENT
E. A MUSICAL INSTRUMENT

**39**

Which of the following is not a dance?

A. BEGUINE
B. PERCALINE
C. TARANTELLA
D. FARRANDOLE
E. POLONAISE

Each of the nine squares in the grid marked 1A to 3C should incorporate all of the items which are shown in the squares of the same letter and number, at the left and top, respectively. For example, 2B should incorporate all of the symbols that are in squares 2 and B. One square, however, is incorrect. Which one is it?

40

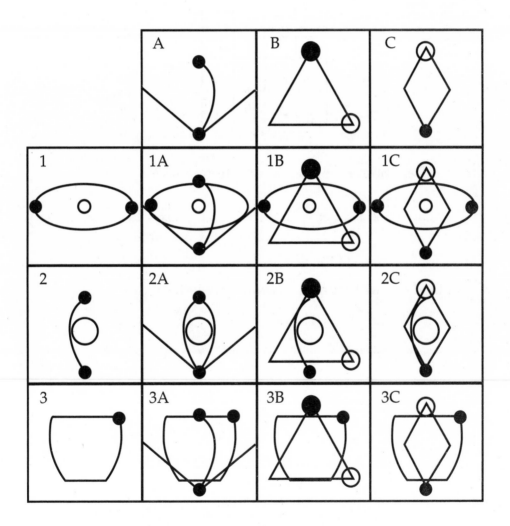

**41**

Which two words are the closest in meaning?

A. MAGNIFICENT
B. VITUPERATIVE
C. SOLEMN
D. DEFAMATORY
E. BRISK
F. MALIGNANT

**42**

| 7 | 14 | 3 | 7 |
| 8 | 23 | 5 | 17 |
| 9 | 21 | 3 | 6 |
| 6 | 20 | 5 | ? |

What number should replace the question mark?

**43**

TOURED FIT is an anagram of what nine-letter word?

**44**

What is a PUNKAH?

A. A FISH
B. A SMOKING IMPLEMENT
C. A FAN
D. A FERN
E. A SERVANT

Each of the nine squares in the grid marked 1A to 3C should incorporate all of the items which are shown in the squares of the same letter and number, at the left and top, respectively. For example, 1B should incorporate all of the symbols that are in squares 1 and B. One square, however, is incorrect. Which one is it?

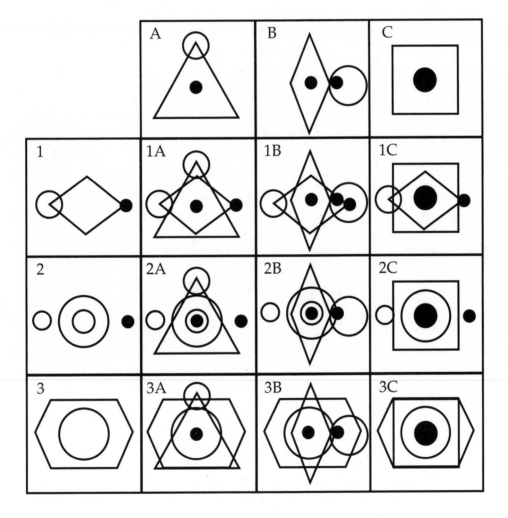

What number should replace the question mark?

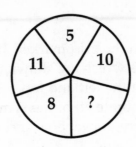

Which of the following is not a weapon?

**A. OERLIKON**
**B. DRUGGET**
**C. SJAMBOK**
**D. HARQUEBUS**
**E. CLAYMORE**

What number should replace the question mark?

1    10   26   ?    87   136

What is a COLLOP?

**A. A SLICE OF MEAT**
**B. A MEDICINE**
**C. A BLOW TO THE HEAD**
**D. A DUSTBIN**
**E. A MEDAL**

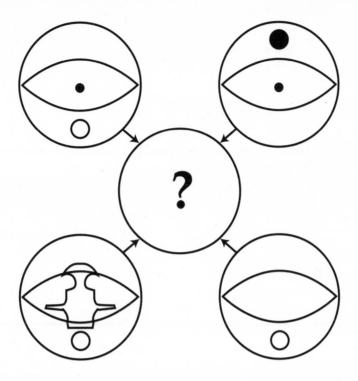

Each line and symbol that appears in the four outer circles, above, is transferred to the middle circle according to how many times it appears, as follows:

**One time — it is transferred**
**Two times — it is possibly transferred**
**Three times — it is transferred**
**Four times — it is not transferred**

Which of the circles below should appear as the middle circle?

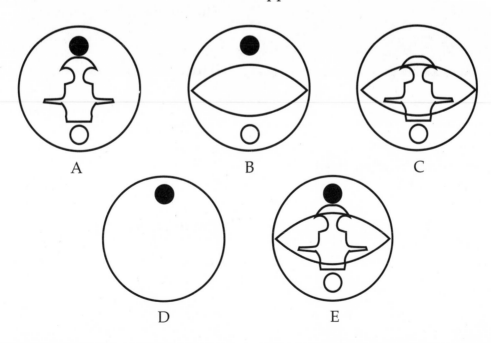

# Answers

**1** Native and ethnic.

**2** D (fist).

All words have letters in the correct alphabetical order without repeating.

**3** 1595.

Reverse the digits and add it to the original to make the next number.

31 + 13 = 44; 44 + 44 = 88; 88 + 88 = 176; 671 + 176 = 847; 748 + 847 = 1595.

**4** B (soft, which is quiet in tone).

The others are all specifically tuneful or pleasant.

**5** D.

**6** Manipulative.

The missing letters are, reading from top to bottom, P, T, and V.

**7** D. The others are exactly the same figure rotated.

**8** Improvidence.

**9** 148.

Reverse the digits in the outer numbers and add them together.

74 + 13 + 61 = 148.

The others are

12 + 23 + 41 = 76; 51 + 26 + 42 = 119.

**10** Heroic.

The letters are: stout**H**earted, f**E**arless, int**R**epid, d**O**ughty, val**I**ant, **C**ourageous.

**11** A (large, which is big).

The others mean general.

**12** B (drum).

A tambour is a type of drum as a clavier is a type of piano.

**13** 5.5.

The sequence is: ÷ 3, + 3, x 3, – 3.
1.5 ÷ 3 = 0.5; 0.5 + 3 = 3.5; 3.5 x 3 = 10.5;
10.5 – 3 = 7.5; 7.5 ÷ 3 = 2.5; 2.5 + 3 = 5.5.

# Answers

**14** ▸ End, to make offend and endanger.

**15** ▸ 40 mph.

180 miles at 40 mph = 4 hours, 30 min; 180 miles at 45 mph = 4 hours.

**16** ▸ G.

Reading across columns and down rows, unique elements in the first two are transferred to the third (bottom or right). Common elements disappear.

**17** ▸ B (pious) and D (irreverent).

**18** ▸ Flotsam and jetsam.

**19** ▸ 6.

(6 x 5 = 30; 6 – 2 = 4; 6 x 2 = 12; 6 + 5 = 11; 6 ÷ 2 =3).

|   | 12 |   |   |   |
|---|----|---|----|---|
|   |    |   |    |   |
| 3 | 4  |   | 30 |   |
|   |    |   |    |   |
|   | ⑥  |   | 11 |   |
|   |    |   |    |   |

**20** ▸ Frequent.

**21** ▸ B (gauche).

**22** ▸ C, a circle is outside and a triangle is in the middle. The others all have the same figure on the outside and in the middle.

**23** ▸ ALmoST, STriDE, DEsiRE, REviLE, LEthAL.

**24** ▸ B (request).

**25** ▸ Jamboree and carnival.

The missing letters are J and B (jamboree) and N and V (carnival).

**26** ▸ A (a mountain nymph).

**27** ▸ 0.625. The lowest common multiple of 8, 12, and 6 is 24, so redo the sum as

$$\frac{21 + 14 - 20}{24}$$

$^{15}/_{24} = {}^{5}/_{8}$, which is 0.625

# Answers

**28** E (GONEDUD or dudgeon, a fish). The others are LIGWATA (wagtail), KYSRLAK (skylark), RAWSOPR (sparrow), and KITRALT (titlark).

**29** Consummate.

**30** C.

At each stage the black circle rotates 135° clockwise, the white circles both rotate 90° clockwise, and the dot with a line rotates 45° clockwise.

**31** B (maunder) and D (meander).

**32** 60.

The sums are
(top left x top right x bottom left) ÷ bottom right = middle.

(9 x 5 x 4) [180] ÷ 3 = 60.

The others are

(6 x 3 x 7) [126] ÷ 2 = 63;
(8 x 4 x 9) [288] ÷ 4 = 72.

**33** C (rayful).

**34** B (flummery, a sweet dessert or porridge).

**35** A.

**36** 8.

The sum of all diagonally opposite segments is 19.

**37** Brazil.

**38** A (a Turkish dish).

**39** B (percaline, a cloth).

**40** 1A.

**41** B (vituperative) and F (malignant).

**42** 10.

Reading across each line, the sums are (first column x third column) – second column = fourth column.
(6 x 5) [30] – 20 = 10.

The others are

(7 x 3) [21] – 14 = 7;
(8 x 5) [40] – 23 = 17;
(9 x 3) [27] – 21 = 6.

# Answers

**43** ▶ Fortitude.

**44** ▶ C (a fan).

**45** ▶ 2B.

**46** ▶ 1.

Start at 11 and read alternate segments clockwise, the sums are – 1, – 2, – 3, and – 4, respectively.

**47** ▶ B (drugget, a type of cloth).

**48** ▶ 51.
At each stage add $3^2$, $4^2$, $5^2$, $6^2$, and $7^2$.
$1 + 3^2$ [9] = 10;
$10 + 4^2$ [16] = 26;
$26 + 5^2$ [25] = 51;
$51 + 6^2$ [36] = 87;
$87 + 7^2$ [49] = 136.

**49** ▶ A (a slice of meat).

**50** ▶ A.

# Notes